The
TAVERN *at the* FERRY

Books by Edwin Tunis

THE TAVERN AT THE FERRY

CHIPMUNKS ON THE DOORSTEP

THE YOUNG UNITED STATES

SHAW'S FORTUNE

COLONIAL CRAFTSMEN

FRONTIER LIVING

INDIANS

COLONIAL LIVING

WHEELS

WEAPONS

OARS, SAILS AND STEAM

The
TAVERN *at the* FERRY

EDWIN TUNIS

Illustrated by the author

THOMAS Y. CROWELL COMPANY

NEW YORK

LIBRARY OF CONGRESS CATALOGING IN PUBLICATION DATA
TUNIS, EDWIN, 1897–
THE TAVERN AT THE FERRY.

SUMMARY: DESCRIBES THE DEVELOPMENT OF SETTLEMENTS,
TAVERNS, AND FERRY CROSSINGS ALONG THE PENNSYLVANIA AND
NEW JERSEY SHORES OF THE DELAWARE RIVER AND THE EVENTS
LEADING TO WASHINGTON'S CROSSING OF THIS RIVER IN 1776.
1. PENNSYLVANIA—SOCIAL LIFE AND CUSTOMS—COLONIAL
PERIOD—JUV. LIT. 2. TRENTON, BATTLE OF,
1776—JUV. LIT. [1. PENNSYLVANIA—SOCIAL
LIFE AND CUSTOMS—COLONIAL PERIOD. 2. TRENTON, BATTLE
OF, 1776] I. TITLE.
F152.T92   917.49′03′2   73–4488
ISBN 0–690–00099–5
1 2 3 4 5 6 7 8 9 10

Contents

BULLFROG

Foreword

IN THE MAIN this is a true story. Its principal characters—the Bakers, the Coryells, the Doans, the Taylors, and some others—were real people. Some minor characters are either wholly fictional or else partly fictional in that real people are assigned small roles that they are not known to have played. Something of the same sort applies to the delineation of early places: the Baker ferry house for instance. It is known to have existed, and where it stood is known, but no picture or description of it has been found. So it has had to be invented on a basis of reasonable conjecture, and on what is known to have been true elsewhere under similar conditions. Where real History occurs, accepted texts have been followed, except that a little unproven tradition appears barefaced with the facts.

Tavern signs appear as ornaments to chapter headings and elsewhere in the book. Though the names on them are those of actual taverns, the symbols are invented. A few such signs survive. They are defaced by weather and time, and the workmanship on them is primitive. To attempt to draw these characteristics is fruitless and tasteless.

Prime among those who have given needed aid in gathering information for this small work is Mrs. William A. Decker, Librarian Emeritus of the Bucks County Historical Society. Mrs. Decker unearthed such a mass of fascinating facts that, without any intention of doing so, she came near to sidetracking the book into a history of the Baker family and its connections. If you think it now is that, you are wrong. For other varied help and comfort, thanks are offered to Mr. Horace Alexander, of Swarthmore, Pennsylvania; to Mr. Sol Feinstone, of Upper Makefield Township, Pennsylvania; to Mr. E. William Fisher, Superintendent of Washington Crossing State Park, Pennsylvania; to Mrs. Ives Goddard, of Harvard University, Cambridge, Massachusetts; to Mrs. J. Robert James, of Wallingford, Pennsylvania; to Mr. Iddo W. Lamtton, General Secretary, Sons of Revolution, New York City; to Mr. and Mrs. W. W. Mac Vicar, of Bethlehem, Pennsylvania; to Dr. Vernon Nelson, Archivist, Moravian College, Bethlehem, Pennsylvania; to Mr. Dirk van Dommelen, Superintendent of Washington Crossing State Park, New Jersey; to Mr. Paul Voorhis, of Nishnawabe Institute, Toronto, Canada; and to Dr. Kemble Widmer, State Geologist for New Jersey, Trenton.

My wife, Elizabeth, has made valuable suggestions in the direction of clarity.

E. T.

Long Last
September 22, 1972

viii

The
TAVERN *at the* FERRY

THE PLOUGH

1.

Quakers in the Woods

EARLY one morning in May 1687, Henry Baker, stepping out of his door, heard a shout from across the river. He walked to the edge of the bank and stood waiting for more information.

"Can ye get me across?" yelled a stranger.

Henry paused a moment before he shouted, "Yes!" He turned away and shouted again, "Tom!"

"Ho," said Tom Canby and came from the stable at a trot.

"Will thee bring that man across the river in the canoe."

"His horse . . ."

"He can lead his horse and it will swim. Require him to lie down in the boat, so that he will not overset it."

"I can try," said Thomas. "I hope he can swim, too."

He walked along the top of the bank and down the sloping path to where a long narrow dugout, made by the local Indians, lay behind an island in the river. He launched the canoe, knelt in it, paddled around the lower end of the island, and turned upstream, fifty feet or

so, to take advantage of an eddy. Then he headed across, keeping his paddle on the downriver side in an effort to keep the strong current from carrying him downstream. Even so, he landed several yards below his passenger and had to work the boat up to where the man stood: a thin figure in buckskin breeches, a loose, rumpled, and soiled homespun coat, and a Montiero cap, its brim peaked in front and turned up behind. He was still on the younger side of forty, with a cheerful leathery face and a gap where two upper front teeth had been.

"How does thee, friend?" said Tom as he landed. "Can thee swim?"

"I'm well enough, thankee, and I can swim. Y'be a Quaker?"

"Aye, like most in these parts. And what is thee?"

"Josh Hartle. Can ye git me across in that thing?"

"I think so, but it's no wherry. Lead thy nag into the water, hold on to his rein, and lie down in the bottom of the boat. That way the horse may tip us over but thee can't."

"How about puttin' me saddlebags in? Want to keep me tools dry."

"All right. Hand 'em over."

The horse appeared to have swum rivers before; he made no difficulty about entering the water and struck out so strongly behind the dugout that he put no drag whatever on it. Tom again paddled on the lower side, trying to head upstream, but, because of the passenger supine in the stern, he now had to kneel in the middle of the boat and his best efforts could not keep the bow headed up. They landed some yards below the Baker house and had to walk up the shore, the stranger leading his horse and Thomas towing the canoe back to its berth.

Henry Baker, short and solid, stood waiting at the top of the path. He wore a broadbrimmed black hat with a domed crown. Below his hat, slightly grizzled hair hung to the shoulders of a straight black coat. He called this coat a tunic; it was of a style thought of as Persian when Charles II introduced it twenty years earlier. Its cuffed sleeves were quite short and revealed half a forearm's

length of Henry's white linen shirtsleeves. The tunic buttoned up to the neck, where the two ends of a plain white linen band fell over it. Henry's stockings were gray worsted; his stout shoes with wide tongues were tied with a short thong, called a latchet.

"Greetings, friend, I am Henry Baker. I'm glad thee had a successful voyage."

"Right tricky craft ye got there, but we made it. I'm Josh Hartle, journeyman coppersmith. Been in Boston, been in New York; goin' to try Philadelphy now."

"Why did thee come this way, instead of by the King's Path to the Falls? There's a ferry there."

"Feller at th' ordinary in Elizabeth Town said 'twas shorter this way. Trail run clean out back there a piece, but I just kep' on acomin' 'til I hit the river."

"Is thee a good coppersmith?"

"Middlin'."

"There is some tinker's work thee could do here. If thee will stop with us a day or two, thee can have food and a bed, and I will pay thee in money for thy work."

Hartle's eyes opened wider. Money was scarce; most farmers paid in produce. This had value, but it was bulky and hard to carry.

* * *

The river was the Delaware. Henry Baker's house stood near it on land that, only three years earlier, had been primeval forest, almost untouched since the last glacier melted. Settlers, pushing quickly into the land that William Penn had bought from the Indians in 1682, had stayed near the river-bank, advancing steadily upstream. So, though the Bakers had English neighbors to the south of them, the only human beings for many miles north were Indians.

The Baker family, though but thirty miles from the new town of Philadelphia, were as

Josh Hartle and Henry Baker

surely pioneers as the solitary hunters who would shortly trudge westward toward the mountains. Henry was a genuine frontiersman, but with major differences: he had no need to seek his fortune—he had brought it with him. And he certainly was not solitary. As companions he had his wife, Margaret, six of their nine children, and ten fellow Quakers. These last were friends and neighbors back in Lancashire, England, who had been unable to raise the five pounds that

would pay their passage to America. So Henry had paid it for them and they had agreed to repay the debt by working four or five years for him. Though none of them seems to have signed the usual bond, these people were officially "indentured servants." Their terms of service had been decided by the Friends Monthly Meeting after they reached Pennsylvania. Tom Canby was one of them; he was also Henry's nephew.

The Society of Friends, called Quakers (derisively at first), was a still-new religious sect. Though its members were devout Christians, their forms of worship and their ways of life were radically different from those of conservative Englishmen, who embalmed old customs and left decisions on religious matters to the clergy. The Friends interpreted spiritual things for themselves. They believed there was in every man an "inner light" that was God's direct communication to him. He had only to wait patiently upon it and it would tell him God's will in all matters. A consensus of these revelations led the Friends to a concern for plainness and simplicity. They avoided all ostentation and ornamentation in their houses and their dress. They rejected all worldly titles, even the simple "Mister." They refused to bear arms, even in self-defense; and they refused to take any oath, or to remove their hats in court, or in the presence of any authority, including the king. Their "plain language" was chiefly direct speech, with "thee" (in early days "thou" also) and "thy" used instead of "you" and "your." All of these "outlandish" things, and even their rule of absolute probity, helped to make them unpopular and suspected. To their neighbors, and to the authorities, they seemed determined to undermine the Established Church, the Army and Navy, and worse, the traditional system of graft. So they were ridiculed, abhorred, and harshly persecuted. Also, even though they did not attend the Anglican Church, each of them was compelled to contribute one tenth of his income for its support.

3

William Penn was a Quaker. When Charles II gave him Pennsylvania, as an easy way out of a debt, Penn offered it as a refuge for Quakers and "an asylum to the good and oppressed of every nation." Many, like Henry Baker's "servants," could not pay their own way; others, who could pay, were mostly artisans—blacksmiths, carpenters, weavers, and so on—but not a few were middle-class farmers, called yeomen, who converted their ancestral lands into cash and risked it all for the privilege of worshipping unmolested in their own way.

Such a yeoman was Henry Baker, who arrived in Philadelphia on the ship *Vine,* July 17, 1684. He bought 300 acres of land from Penn in what would become Makefield Township, Bucks County. He paid forty shillings an acre, plus one shilling an acre yearly as quit rent "forever." Payment of quit rent was an acknowledgment of allegiance. Failure to pay it gave the landlord a theoretical right to repossess the land.

Henry had help for the arduous job of clearing the forest, but, even so, the larger trees were too big to be felled with axes. They had to be left standing and merely "deadened" by chopping away their bark in a band that encircled the trunk. Woodworkers came out from Philadelphia to shape the best of the smaller logs into timbers and planks for a house. Other logs, left rough, served to build a stable, a bunkhouse, and some small cabins for the married couples. All these outbuildings were "blockhouses," as the English then called the log cabins that they copied from Swedish ones along the lower Delaware. The roofs of the blockhouses were thatched with rushes.

As nearly as he could, Henry duplicated the farmhouse he had left behind in England. He placed the new one at the top of the slope that rises from the crest of the steep riverbank. A modern house would probably face the water; this one turned a gable end to it. Like the English house, the new one had four rooms, two on each floor, and two large chimneys, one at each end; but those chimneys were brick and these were stone. Like the English roof, this one was steep and its eaves came well down below the level of the second-story ceiling; but that roof was thatched with straw, while this one was covered with "shakes," hand-split from short logs. They were put on rough and lapped like shingles.

Like the Lancashire one, the Pennsylvania house was framed with stout oak timbers held together by mortise-and-tenon joints with long wooden pins through them. As in the old house, the spaces between the timbers of the new one were filled with "nogging." But in England the nogging was bricks and mortar, exposed to the weather; here it was cobblestones from the river, bedded in clay, and covered on the outside with feather-edge clapboards split from logs, like the shakes. Pine boards, planed smooth, covered the inside walls; and the low ceilings were nothing more than the undersides of the wide planks that floored the rooms overhead.

Builders in London and even in Philadelphia had begun to give more attention to making the outsides of houses symmetrical than to the convenient arrangement of the rooms inside. If simple country people like the Bakers knew about this, they paid no attention to it. They went on arranging their rooms to suit themselves and placing doors and windows wherever they would best serve their purpose. Warm rooms were more important than well-lighted ones; so the house had but eight windows, all fitted with leaded casements—two in each room, upstairs and down. The Bakers' one entrance door stood considerably to the right of the middle of the house to permit it to open into one corner of the large "keeping room" that served for living, eating, and cooking. A door on the right, just inside the entrance, led to a smaller room generally called the "parlour." Originally a parlour was a roomlet adjoining the great hall of a castle. This parlour was larger. It had in it an imposing bedstead in-

4

Henry Baker's house

tended for the use of guests but ordinarily occupied by the sturdy form of Deborah Booth, who was housekeeper and mother's helper. A rough homemade bed frame, standing against the room's front wall, provided a sleeping place for Deb's special charges: the Bakers' young sons, Samuel and Nathan. Margaret Baker's loom was set up near the rear window of this room; and her two spinning wheels, a small one for flax and a large one for wool, stood against a wall. All three remained idle for a couple of years until the farm could grow raw material for their use.

Much of the furniture in the keeping room had come from the Lancashire farm. It suggested utility, not comfort. A long oak table stood a little more than a stool's width out from the front wall, with Henry Baker's straight-backed armchair at its fireplace end. On Henry's right an equally stiff chair with-

out arms was reserved for Margaret. Stools and benches were seats for Deb and the three older daughters. The youngest daughter, Esther, and the two boys ate standing and silent at the foot of the table. The Bakers were not stern parents, but rules were rules and this was the way things were done.

Several square joint-stools, all black with age and all different, were moved about the room as they were needed. No one moved the tall oak settle that stood by the fireplace as it had in England for several generations of Bakers. Its narrow seat, a mere shelf, gave no comfort, but its straight back provided a welcome shelter from drafts on cold nights. This back was so tall that its top missed the joists of the ceiling by inches. Just below its top it supported a long low cupboard with two doors, each carved with a formalized representation of linen in stiff vertical folds.

5

Deb had to stand on tiptoe to reach the flitches of bacon that were stored behind the doors.

Nothing was more plentiful here than fuel, so each of the four rooms had a fireplace. The largest of these, by far, not only warmed the keeping room but also cooked all the meals. It was seven feet wide and three feet deep, and its hearth of flat stones extended another three feet into the room. Shoulder-high above the hearth, a heavy oaken manteltree spanned the opening and carried the weight of the stonework above it. Behind this beam, and parallel to it, a forged iron bar supported the hooks from which Deb hung iron pots over the fire to boil food. The length of these hooks, called trammels, could be adjusted to control the speed of the cooking. Lugs on the heavy andirons supported the long iron spits on which the Bakers roasted their meat. The spits had a crank at one end, and it was ten-year-old Samuel's despised job to turn them slowly, so that the meat would cook evenly on all sides. The juices of the meat dripped into a flat pan on the hearth, and at intervals Deb would dip up some of it with a long-handled spoon and baste the meat.

To save the cook from much stooping and from having to work too close to the fire, all the utensils, except the stew pots, had long handles. The pots and skillets were cast iron; all the rest—the forks, the dippers, the strainers, the gridiron (for broiling)—were wrought iron. All the utensils stayed within reach around the fireplace. Some were hung on pegs driven into the manteltree, others simply sat on the hearth until they were needed. Tableware—a few pottery jugs and pitchers, and pewter plates, bowls, and tankards—stood on shelves fastened to the wooden wainscot. The girls polished the pewter once a week with wood-ashes and water. The Bakers used iron knives and pewter spoons at the table, but no forks. Fingers served instead, and were wiped on linen napkins. These were large enough to cover the user's clothes down to his knees when tied around his neck. Fresh napkins appeared at every meal. The meals, by the way, were breakfast at ten, dinner at two, and supper at six. These people rose early, had a morning draft of ale or cider, and did four hours' work before breakfast.

Inside the fireplace, on the left about two feet above the hearth, was the oven where Deb baked bread twice a week. The oven was itself a small fireplace, about a foot and a half wide, with an arched ceiling, and quite deep. It had a flue of its own that vented into the main chimney. On baking days Deb kept a hot fire of small sticks burning in the oven for several hours, while her loaves were rising. By the time they were ready, the stones surrounding the oven were heated through. Deb raked out the embers of her fire, swept

Trammel

The keeping room

the ashes from the oven floor, and slid her round loaves in with a long-handled wooden shovel, called a peel. She then closed the front of the oven with a wooden door and left the bread to bake slowly all night. The crust of bread baked this way was hard and much thicker than modern crust, but the bread was also much better than modern bread.

In the back corner of the keeping room, opposite the front door, a narrow stair wound upward, leading to the large chamber which served as a dormitory for the four Baker daughters. A door near the head of the steps led into the bedroom of Henry and Margaret. To these people, bedrooms were for sleeping; only in sickness did they occupy them in the daytime. As a result, the rooms were sparsely furnished. Their floors were bare, as were all the floors in the house. The girls slept on two bed frames, made on the place, like the one their brothers used. Two lidded chests for sheets and blankets, two stools with spokeshaved legs and round seats, and a very small looking-glass in a heavy walnut frame made the total of the furniture in the dormitory. Pegs, set in boards on the wall, took the place of closets for clothes.

The room of the senior Bakers, though smaller, was a little more elaborate. In addition to the pegs, the looking-glass, and the stools, there was a single chest which boasted two drawers under its lidded compartment. Alongside the window against the front wall, a small stand held a pewter basin on its top; a ewer of the same metal stood on a shelf under it. The four tall posts of the oak bedstead, ancient even then, supported a cornice that barely missed the ceiling. In fact, the ceiling had been built to fit the bed. White linen curtains hung from the inner faces of the cornice. These were drawn entirely around the sleepers at night. The "spring" of stretched rope that supported a featherbed was so high above the floor that a wooden step was needed for getting up onto it. The bed was too short for an adult to stretch out at full length, so the Bakers reclined on it, leaning against large pillows. Everybody slept this way at the time.

All that the Bakers did was of intense interest to the Indians of a small "town" known as Winnahawchunick. It consisted of a dozen or so dome-shaped *wigiwams,* enclosed by a circular palisade, standing on the riverbank about four miles upstream from the farm. Its inhabitants were a small band belonging to the Turtle clan of the great tribe which the English named the Delawares. They called themselves Lenni Lenape, "true men." They were fine people—generous and kind. Though a later generation of whites cheated the Indians and angered them, the Lenape never broke the agreements they made with William Penn. The Bakers never had any fear of Indian attack and they never were attacked, nor were any other Quakers, even when the Lenape fought against the English in the French and Indian War. Henry found them good neighbors and he treated them accordingly. He bought game and fish from them, and pelts, which he could resell at a profit in Philadelphia. He paid the Indians with good blankets and iron tools. It was they who hollowed out the big tulip log to make the canoe in which Tom ferried Josh Hartle across the river.

Only by slow degrees did Henry's workers convert the forest into a self-supporting and, finally, a profitable farm. Henry made James Yates, who came over with him, the farm manager because he himself was often away from home on public business. He was a member of the Provincial Assembly and was foreman of the first grand jury in Bucks County. At that time the grand jury functioned as a county council, setting the boundaries of townships and opening new roads. Henry was also a close friend and adviser of William Penn.

James Yates planted crops between the

Henry Baker's earmark

skeletons of the deadened trees and steadily enlarged the fields. The clearing yielded an enormous amount of excess wood. James loaded firewood and some good timber on oxcarts and hauled it down below the lowest rapids of the rivers. From there it could travel by water to Philadelphia. The trash wood that remained was burned in great heaps, reducing it to ashes, from which James extracted potash. This he sent to town on the backs of packhorses. In summer, if they were not working, these horses ran loose in the woods to browse; so did all of the Baker cows and pigs; so did the cows, pigs, and horses, of the neighbors (every year brought more of them). To avoid arguments, each owner had a mark that he cut into an ear, sometimes both ears, of his animals. Phineas Pemberton, the Clerk of the County, recorded the earmarks in a book. Each entry shows a diagram of the mark, with a written description under it—except for Henry Baker's earliest mark, dated 1684, which shows only the diagram. In 1696 Henry registered another earmark, described as: "A slit in the top of the nearer [left] & a half-penny cut under, on the same ear."

* * *

The Bakers and their retainers lived on one of the extreme edges of European civilization, but they never forgot they were Quakers. On First Days (Sundays), if the weather allowed it, nearly everybody on the place rode on horseback and in oxcarts to Weekly Meeting at William Yardley's or Richard Hough's—a slow journey of four or five miles southward. Even at a Meeting held in a private house, the Friends followed their custom of having the men sit on the left side of the room and the women on the right. They entered regular Meeting Houses through separate doors. Yet, from the first, women were the full equals of men in the Society. The men kept their hats on in Meeting. A few acknowledged leaders, called elders, sat along the front wall facing the congregation. In most Meeting Houses a platform called the gallery was provided for them. Though certain elders, men or women, were "recorded ministers," there was no officiating clergyman. The congregation waited in silence for the Spirit of the Lord to move someone to speak. This could be anyone, man or woman. Sometimes no one spoke at all, yet the members could leave content that it had been a "good Meeting" because of the spiritual unity they had felt and their sense of the presence of the Lord.

The Society of Friends had (and has) an interesting system of government. From its beginning through the early nineteen-hundreds, the Meeting had to approve all the marriages—in fact, all the actions—of its members. Anyone who stepped aside from the straight path was expected to confess his fault publicly and promise to do better in the future. Henry Baker, an elder of the Falls Meeting, was reprimanded by it for having bought a Negro slave.

Many American Quakers were slave owners in early times, though they treated their slaves as fellow humans. Almost from the first some Friends felt a "concern" about slave owning and especially about the buying and selling of men and women. They moved their Meetings to take stronger and stronger stands against the practice. Many Quakers freed their slaves as a matter of conscience, but in the South they hesitated to do so because freeing them would amount to cruelty. Unscrupulous men would recapture the Negroes and resell them to masters who would mistreat them. The Friends abstained from buying or selling slaves for many years before they resolved, in 1776, that any Quaker who owned a slave would be disowned by his Meeting.

As at the original Yearly Meeting in Lon-

Quaker Meeting

don, all members were free to participate in business sessions. No vote was taken; people spoke for or against a proposal until the Clerk, or chairman, perceived a consensus, which he recorded. If there was an obvious division of opinion, the subject was postponed for future discussion. In America some matters, like the slavery question, stayed unsettled for years.

Each "Particular Meeting," as local Weekly Meetings were called, sent delegates to a Monthly Meeting which united several Particular Meetings. Representatives of the Monthly Meetings attended a Quarterly Meeting that might include a whole county. (A Quarterly Meeting was held at Richard Hough's in June 1685.) The Quarterly Meetings in turn delegated members to the Yearly Meetings, which were concerned with still larger areas. Before the end of the seventeenth century, there were several Yearly Meetings in the colonies.

2.

Bakers Ferry

THE YEAR is 1693. Before sunrise on a chilly October morning the slope in front of the Baker house is churning with what looks like a confusion of packhorses. Drivers are tightening girths and checking pack hitches; clad in white smocks, farmers, who own some of the horses and the burdens they carry, are getting in the drivers' way and issuing unnecessary instructions. Twenty-seven of the horses belong to Henry Baker; some sixty more are owned in varying numbers by his neighbors. All have gathered here to make up a long train that will carry their wheat crop to Philadelphia. This Bucks County land grows fine wheat, and an acre of it yields twice what an acre of the best English land will grow.

Henry's horses are burdened with more

Henry Baker and Joseph Milnor

than two tons of grain. Each horse carries 160 pounds in two coarse linen sacks, lashed to a packsaddle and covered with a square tarpaulin as a protection against rain. Wet wheat is not saleable. This pack train is not only the longest that this neighborhood has yet assembled, it will also be the first to strike directly through the forest to Philadelphia, by way of Newtown, instead of using the longer trail along the bank of the Delaware. Seventeen-year-old Samuel Baker and Aaron Rundle, Yates's right-hand man, who will lead the train, have explored the new trail and found that, as Gabriel Thomas wrote: "A Cart or Wain may go through the middle of the Woods between the Trees without getting any damage." But no wains yet exist in Makefield Township, and the few carts are rigged to be drawn by oxen, needed for other work at home.

Without too much excitement, the unshod horses are assembled into six strings of fourteen or fifteen animals. Each string has a mounted leader, to whose saddle the halter rope of the first packhorse is fastened. Each of these lead horses wears a bell hung on a strap around his neck. Aaron raises a hand in salute and starts the first string off to-

ward the southwest at an easy walk. Sam Baker, proud but determinedly casual at the head of the second string, also salutes his father and Joseph Milnor, who watch near the door of the house. As the tinkling of the bells dies away, the sun rises beyond the river. The farmers ride off homeward, taking their misgivings with them, and Henry Baker says, " 'Tis a thirsty business, watching other men work! Come in, Joseph, and drink a can of cider with me. It is still new, but it is good. Mary will have breakfast for us shortly. We are all hungry. We've been about for three hours."

"Thank thee, Henry. Mary makes thee a good wife."

"Aye. She is content, I think; and I am, though she is not Margaret."

"Thee has named thy new daughter Margaret?"

"Aye. Mary would have it so."

The two men seat themselves at the corner of the long table near the fire, and Esther Baker brings them their cider in large pewter pots.

"Thee is right, it is good."

"Joseph," says Henry, "We have a quandary. Travelers have worn a path to the riverbank over there. They are forever shouting to be brought across. It takes time and trouble and there is some danger in it. Can thee think what we can do about it?"

"Well, it has become known that this way is shorter than the road by the falls, and that thee has a boat. Why does thee not charge them for passage?"

"In such a cockle as that? It can carry but two men, and them perilously. I will not ride in the thing; if a man but turn his head too quickly, he finds himself in the river!"

"Hold a moment, Henry. Once, long ago, a sailor in Blackpool told me of islanders in the Southern Ocean who join two narrow boats like yours side by side to make a craft that even great seas cannot overset. Could thee get another canoe?"

"I think I could," Henry says, staring down

the table and tilting his forearms, held parallel before him. "And I think I see what thee means. We could build a deck across them, and charge a penny for a man and another for his horse."

"Breakfast," says Esther, as she places a spoon and a bowl of mush and boiled bacon before each man.

* * *

It took the Indians about a month to hollow out the new dugout, and when it was finished it was about a foot shorter than the old one. This made no important difference, however, and ten days later the new ferryboat stood ready to use. Its builders had never heard the word "catamaran"—nor "pirogue," as such a craft was called on the Mississippi River a hundred years later; they simply called their contraption "the ferry." Whatever its name, it served its purpose. The two narrow hulls slipped easily through the water, and the five-foot space between them removed all tendency to tip over.

The ferry's deck was fourteen feet long and little over eight feet wide, with a low railing along both sides. Paddling it was impractical, but Tom Canby, who stayed on as ferryman, learned the tricks of poling it so well that he could hit the landings on either side almost every time. Tom had finished his term of service five years ago but had continued to work on the place to build up his capital. He and Sally Jarvis had been married only a few months at the time the ferry was finished. In another year he would leave to start out on his own.

At the end of a crossing, Tom landed the boat by simply grounding its forward end on the shore and then thrusting his pole into the river bottom to keep the current from sweeping the boat away. Two parallel boards with cleats across them made a gangplank for bringing horses aboard. One of these lay on each shore. Most horses could be led on easily, but now and then a nervous nag had to be blindfolded. Tom kept all horses in the middle of the boat by tying them to both rails with ropes fastened to their bridles. An unmounted passenger had no need of the gang-

plank; he could put a foot on the end of the longer dugout and step aboard, usually giving the boat a shove off as he did so. Travelers wishing to cross from the Jersey side blew a blast on a horn that Henry had hung on a tree. Soon the "road" from Newtown led to "Bakers Ferry," and continued beyond it into New Jersey and to Manhattan. Bakers Ferry kept the name for eighty years.

Most of Tom's time was devoted to ferrying. Many a traveler, lacking the penny or two that would pay his fare, worked out the cost of his passage at some farm chore. And many a one, arriving at dusk, was freely given a pallet in the farmhands' bunkhouse and went his way in the morning with a breakfast under his belt.

Three years after Henry Baker started the ferry, he and Mary left the farm in the hands of James Yates and young Samuel and moved to Bristol, the county town, twelve miles to the south. There Henry busied himself with provincial and county affairs and became the partner of Samuel Carpenter in the operation of a gristmill and a sawmill. Henry Baker died in Bristol in 1701.

Samuel Baker was twenty-five years old when, being the older son, he inherited the entire Bakers Ferry farm, including 250 acres to the north that his father had added to the original place. All of Samuel's sisters had married and left the farm, and so had Deborah Booth. Nathan, the younger brother, seeing no likely prospects at home, had gone to Philadelphia. Two years after he became a landowner, Samuel married Rachel Warder in the new Falls Meeting House. Rachel had grown up in Bristol, and Samuel found her when he went there to visit his father and stepmother. No ritual marked a Quaker wedding. Samuel and Rachel, having received the Meeting's permission to marry, simply stood before the congregation and announced in their own words that they were now man and wife. The members of the Meeting who knew them best then signed the Clerk's record book as witnesses. Honeymoon trips had not yet come into fashion. The young couple went directly from their wedding to Bakers Ferry, and Rachel took over the management of the farmhouse at once.

3.

The Ferry House

BOWMANS HILL rises some 300 feet above the level of the river four miles north of Bakers Ferry. It gets its name from a bachelor of some mystery, John Bowman, who built himself a cabin on its north slope before 1700. A man with the same name had served as surgeon on the ship in which Captain William Kidd set out to catch pirates. When the Captain turned pirate himself, so did Doctor Bowman. One of the many yarns about the hiding of Kidd's booty asserts that he and the Doctor brought the gold up the Delaware and buried it on Bowmans Hill. The Doctor stayed, presumably to watch the treasure, while Captain Kidd followed a circuitous route to London and the hangman's noose. Since that time many have dug holes in the hill, but none has admitted finding anything.

When a second man, Jonathan Pidcock, settled on the creek that winds past the north side of Bowmans Hill, the Indians who lived

Pidcock's mill and house (reconstructed)

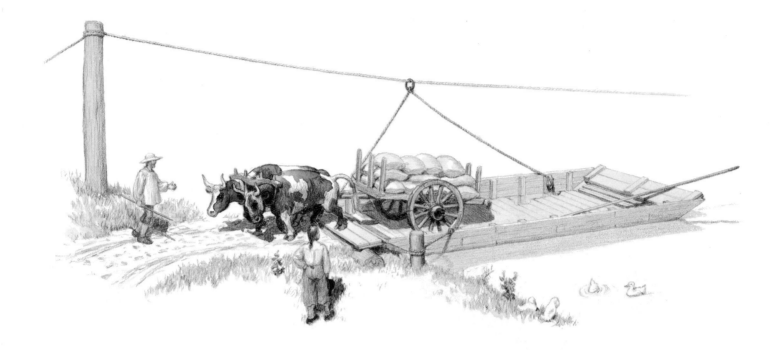

just below the creek began to feel crowded. They abandoned their town, and most of them went north to join others of their clan; but a small band settled inland a few miles, and one squaw moved in with the Bakers.·

In 1702 Pidcock built himself a stone dwelling—the first of its kind in these parts. It still stands as the middle section of a larger, quite notable house. But before Pidcock built it, he and his friend John Bowman started a gristmill, run by the flow of Pidcocks Creek. It was a convenience not only to neighborhood people but also to settlers near the river in New Jersey. Their trips to the mill, with a sack of grain across the back of a horse, increased traffic on Bakers Ferry and extended the "River Road" northward. Soon Pidcock's customers wanted to bring cartloads of sacked grain to his mill, but the double canoe was too small to carry a cart and the oxen that pulled it. The old craft was decaying, anyway, so Samuel built what he called a "skeow" to replace it.

This vessel was a shallow box twenty-two feet long and half as wide. It would float on ten inches of water even when it was loaded with a grain-filled cart and a span of oxen.

The scow's bottom was made of two layers of thick pine planks. The bottom was perfectly flat for most of its length but it sloped upward on both ends to allow the ferry to head in close to the shore. The upper side of the bottom planking served as the deck; nailed across its sloping ends, narrow battens, closely spaced, provided footholds for animals. The low sides of the boat were vertical. Instead of the old gangplanks on the shore, the new ferry had ramps hinged to it across both ends. They could be turned inboard to lie on the battens when the boat was under weigh.

Ben Wilson had taken over as ferryman. When Ben made a landing, he immediately secured the scow close against the shore by hitching two lines that lay there, ready for the purpose, to wooden cleats on the sides of the boat. Then he turned the forward ramp down to rest on a sizable log that lay parallel to the flow of the river to receive it. Stones and earth, banked against the inshore side of the log, created an easy slope for a cart to roll on or off the ferry. Even a skittish horse would come aboard with no more ado than laying his ears back, and oxen just plodded ahead until they were told to stop. The passage of a horse now cost tuppence; an ox-cart, sixpence.

Passage on this boat couldn't be called rapid transit. It took nearly half an hour to cover the 280 yards from shore to shore; but nobody was ever in a hurry. Ben, having raised the ramp (sometimes the passenger did it), cast off the mooring lines and carried his long iron-tipped "settin' pole" to the forward end of the scow. There he rested its tip against the river bottom and, leaning on the pole, walked slowly aft. Actually Ben and his pole stayed in one place while the boat moved forward past the pole. When the stern came up to Ben, he carried his pole forward again and repeated the performance.

This was a "rope ferry," so Ben no longer had to worry about the current carrying him sideways downstream. Both ends of the ferryboat were hitched on the upstream side to an eight-inch iron ring which slid on a stout rope hung above the water from shore to shore. The rope was not taut. Its flat curve sagged between two tall posts so that it cleared the water by a few feet in the middle of the river. The posts were placed just far enough upstream to allow for this sag and for the length of the bridle that connected the boat to the sliding ring. When the long rope tightened in wet weather, Ben had to lengthen the bridle in order to land in the right place.

Rope ferries crossing swift streams where there were no rocks or islands to interfere sometimes made use of a "midstream anchor." This could be a standard forged iron hook, but more often it was a massive weight, or even a stout post. Whatever its character, it was placed in the middle of the river well above the course of the ferry. A stout rope from anchor to boat allowed the ferry to travel through an arc of about fifty degrees from landing to landing without being carried downstream by the current. No information has been found that deals with the problem of attaching a new rope to the anchor when the old one wore out.

Rope ferries of both kinds, or ropeless ferries on sluggish streams, crossed, or would eventually cross, all the wider rivers in the colonies. As population increased, so did the number of ferries. Before the days of long bridges, there was a ferry every four or five miles along the Delaware. Narrower streams, like Houghs Creek and Pidcocks Creek, could be and were readily bridged, first with rough logs, later with hewn timbers, or with stone arches; but wide rivers presented problems that were not solved until near the end of the 1700's. Bridges had crossed wide rivers in Europe for centuries, however.

As traffic increased, the Bakers' kindly custom of feeding benighted wayfarers and giving them a place to sleep became a burden. The occasional woman who turned up had to have special treatment in the way of a bed in the farmhouse, or in one of the farmhands' cabins. Samuel, like his father, never felt above picking up an honest penny of profit wherever he found it. So, since he them someone to talk to—and talk about. Above all, the patrons brought in news of the outside world. After 1704 newspapers appeared in the larger colonial centers, but few of them reached Makefield. The same hunger for news, and the opportunity to meet strangers, led local men to seek excuses for stopping at the ferry house to rest on a bench with a pot of Samuel's cider (one penny) or of Philadelphia ale (tuppence). As they did with all ordinaries connected with ferries, people commonly called Baker's "the ferry house." Wherever a ferry crossed, there was likely to be a ferry house, and often there were two—one on each bank of the river.

The patrons of the Baker ordinary usually found its host dressed, like his farmer neighbors, in a linen work frock, or smock. It was quite full and reached not quite halfway to his knees. Its wide sleeves ended in close-fitting cuffs. The yoke, to which the gown and sleeves were attached, had an opening in its front, to let the wearer get the garment over his head, and was topped by a turn-over collar. Samuel wore his frock over warm woolen clothes in winter, and over nothing above the waist in summer. Below the waist,

was forced into serving the public, he decided to charge for the service. He turned his house into an "ordinary." The only physical change this required was the erection, in the front yard, of a pole with a small bush tied to its top to indicate that food and drink were for sale.

An ordinary differed from a tavern in several ways. However gregarious a tavern keeper might be, his family mixed with the guests little more than serving them required. Quite often the family lived in a house apart from the tavern, or at least in a part of the building to which guests had no access. At a tavern, guests could usually get meals at any time and were offered some choice of what they would eat. An ordinary's patrons moved right in with the family and ate with them whatever simple food was put on the table—at the time the family was ready to eat it. A tavern keeper was supposed to dispense various mixed drinks and to be able to supply a bottle of wine on demand. An ordinary limited itself to cider, ale, and Barbados rum.

Converting their home into a public house wasn't so much of a hardship for the Bakers as you might expect. Though prosperous, they were simple folk, and their visitors gave

Samuel in Philadelphia

in warm weather, he wore linen breeches, linen "thread" stockings, and stout latcheted shoes with square toes. His winter work breeches were buckskin and with them he wore high cowhide boots over knitted woolen stockings. His everyday hats had wide brims and flat-topped crowns; they were made of wool felt in winter, of home-plaited straw in summer.

Samuel was taller than his father had been and was inclined to plumpness. Dressed for Meeting, or seen on the streets of Philadelphia, he was an impressive figure. The oppressions he had suffered in England had put a stern, taut expression on Henry's face; his son, though he had dignity, regarded the world with benign eyes from a round and rosy face and smiled readily. His dress-up clothes, though sober in color and Quaker-plain, were well tailored from the best materials he could get. His wide hat of felted beaver fur cost the equivalent of something like two hundred dollars. One beaver hat was enough for a lifetime. Those Quakers who wore cheaper wool hats often had to "guy" the wide brims with strings passed over the crowns, to keep them from drooping.

Samuel's dark gray coat, which he called sad-colored, buttoned up from waist to throat. It had wider skirts than his father's tunic had had, and larger cuffs, though they were small compared to the cuffs of a Boston merchant or Virginia planter of the time. Samuel Baker wore none of the lace that these gentlemen displayed. The falling ends of the white band he wore around his neck were neatly hemmed and the cuffs of his full-sleeved shirt were unadorned, but both band and shirt were made of the finest linen that Philadelphia afforded. Black breeches reached below his knees to cover the tops of his heavy black silk stockings. The aforementioned gentlemen wore white stockings, which they drew up over their breeches and gartered above the knee. A garter at this time was simply a ribbon tied or buckled around the leg, and it didn't do its job very

well. These elegants wore ribbon bows on their shoes, and above them the shoe tongues rose an unnecessary three inches. Samuel's tongues were long enough to serve their purpose, but no longer, and short leather thongs made all the bows he needed. Among fashionable men, the long curls of the full-bottomed wig were now gathered into a hank at the back and were tied there with a wide ribbon bow, or were stuffed into a silk bag which hung below the bow. Samuel and his fellow Quakers let their shoulder-length hair fall unrestrained.

Rachel Baker was scandalized by the stiffened frontlets that projected six inches ahead of the lace caps of fashionable ladies; by their bunched-up overskirts that displayed an expanse of quilted petticoat; and above all, by their low-cut bodices, not really immodest, but exposing an expanse of chest. Rachel went to the weekly First Day Meeting in a plain linen cap, the short lappets of which she tied in a neat bow under her chin. Her bodice, sleeves, and overskirt were all of the same gray woolen kersey. She laced the bodice up the front and wore a wide white kerchief over it around her shoulders. Her sleeves, neither tight nor full, ended in turned-back cuffs below her elbows. The full sleeves of her white shift showed below the cuffs and were confined with narrow black ribbons above her wrists. Rachel's overskirt met in front at the bottom of her bodice and fell from there, open, straight to the ground, revealing only a glimpse of the petticoat under it. Even at Meeting, she commonly wore a plain white apron that reached to her knees. The clothes Rachel wore daily around the house were much the same except that they were made of coarser, home-woven materials, and her working apron was larger than her First Day one.

For cold weather Rachel had a warm woolen "hood" that was actually a full-length cape with a hood attached to it. Her husband also owned one, quite like hers, which he called a cloak. Neither of them hesitated to

Rachel Baker spinning wool

pull the hood over their heads when necessary and then put on a hat over it. Rachel's hat, broad brimmed and high crowned, was much like the hats still worn by Welsh women when they put on their traditional costume. In passing: the Quaker bonnet shaped like a coal-scuttle, later universally worn by the women of the Society of Friends, did not appear at all until the early years of the 1800's.

* * *

The local importance of the ferry house was increased by the appointment of Samuel Baker to be a Justice of the Peace for Makefield Township. The solid plank door of the ferry house became a bulletin board for official notices and for informal private ones. The Provincial government announced a date for the collection of quit rents; and James Harrison asked any neighbor who saw his bay stallion, with a white patch on his offside shoulder, to hold him and notify James. The Court of Quarter Sessions posted its list of petit jurors on the door; and Thomas Janney announced there that he would sell thirty-seven ewes and a Shropshire ram at a "vendue" in front of the ferry house, and gave the date, Quaker style: "11th month, 15th day, 1710." The year had

been a dry one, so Thomas lacked enough hay to feed his whole flock through the coming winter.

Some settlers who were not Quakers had come to Makefield, and there were also lax Quakers, more "worldly" than was pleasing to the Meeting, which, if persuasion failed, ousted them. Nearly all of both groups were honest and decent people, but now and then somebody stepped over the thou-shalt-not line. It was possible that the disappearance of James Harrison's horse had been assisted. Most offenses were minor ones. One man was accused of murder about this time, less than a dozen miles from the ferry, but he appears to have been acquitted. In so thin a population, where everybody knew everybody, the finger of suspicion was likely to point accurately; and stolen goods were hard to conceal. Most of the transgressors who appeared before Samuel were "prygmen" who had stolen wash from the bushes where a housewife had spread it to dry. A few were horse or cattle thieves, whom Judge Baker could try if the value of their plunder didn't exceed forty shillings. (This would probably include the Harrison stallion.) Above forty shillings the case went to the higher court at Bristol.

Samuel heard evidence and pronounced

sentence in his own kitchen with not too much formality in the process. There was no jail to which a culprit might be committed, though a suspect might be tied up overnight in the bunkhouse to await trial. Occasionally an offender might be lashed, by a temporary court-appointed whipper, for such a fault as beating his wife. The customary sentence for theft was payment to the victim of four times the value of the stolen goods. If the thief could not pay, and few could, he was condemned to work out the value in labor for the person he had injured.

About the time Samuel was made a justice, he was also granted a license to keep a public house—though he was already actively running one. He further received a Provincial franchise to operate a ferry, which again was after the fact. Such anticipations were the general rule. The franchise fixed the hours and weather conditions when the ferry must give service, and also set the maximum charges for service. It also expressly forbade any other ferry to operate within four miles up or down the river. This prohibition was effective for Pennsylvania but could not keep ferries from operating from the New Jersey side.

In addition to dispensing justice, Samuel served as a member of the Provincial Assembly, as his father had before him. It was quite usual in the American colonies that a publican, or tavern keeper, should be an outstanding man. The Governors' Councils preferred to license men known to be respected in their localities and well acquainted with their neighbors and their neighbors' concerns.

The local patrons of the ferry house endlessly discussed the affairs of the township and the province; they had not yet broadened their view to include the problems of the colonies as a whole. Local births, marriages, and deaths; the price of wheat; the need for improved roads; and even the growing commerce of Philadelphia—all these subjects were dealt with around the hearth of the ordinary, and the landlord heard it all and contributed his bit. Most tavern keepers seem to have been cheery and polite (and curious) but never servile as such men were in Europe. Haughty travelers from overseas, expecting and demanding subservience, ran the risk of being asked to leave American taverns and ordinaries, even in these early times. Leaving a hostel at night, in the middle of nowhere, could be inconvenient.

The Bakers made little change in the arrangement of their house, or in their way of life, when they began to keep a public house. Most travelers were content to pay sixpence for supper and a penny to sleep on a pallet in the bunkhouse. An occasional, more affluent guest was charged a shilling to sleep in the parlour but ate the same food and paid the same price for it that everyone else did. Many a wayfarer, who had no money at all and was frank about it, still split firewood or did some other task to pay his scot. The old keeping room had acquired two new armchairs slightly less uncomfortable than Henry's old one, which still kept its place. People called this room the kitchen, though it served as an all-purpose public room. From its old table guests and the family ate; beside its fire they smoked their pipes and toasted their shins, while Rachel and her helpers cooked on the hearth.

Fresh beef and mutton were rarities on the table. The Bakers killed cows and sheep only to cull their stock. When these meats did appear, they were so tough that they had to be stewed to rags to be edible. Fresh pork was common for a while in cold weather; but the farm provided enough salted beef and pork, and enough smoked hams and bacon, to last the year around. The Quakers were not expert hunters; so, when the Indians left, the supply of game dwindled. The clearing of more and more woodland had reduced the population of game anyway; that was the prime reason for the Indians leaving. Though the white men had trouble in killing a deer, or a bear, with a single lead musket ball that tumbled erratically through the air, they did better when they loaded the same gun with a handful of small bird-shot that would spread out when fired at wild ducks, wild geese, swans, and passenger pigeons. All of these passed through, spring and fall, in such incredible numbers that they were hard to miss. The Quakers also did well with fishing—netting shad, salmon, and even sturgeon, all of which at that time came up the river to spawn.

For the rest of the edibles: There were root vegetables (scarce in late winter), always plenty of cornmeal mush and hominy, always cornbread and often wheat or rye bread, often honey, but seldom butter. The Dutch were the butter eaters; a few of the English were just learning to spread it on bread—with their thumbs. The Bakers now drank a lot of tea, some coffee, and even some chocolate; they sweetened all three with bought loaf sugar. They also drank hard cider and beer, and West Indian rum was available at the ferry house. Quakers seldom use alcohol nowadays, but then they drank temperately as a matter of course. Almost all non-Quakers drank, too—many not temperately.

One of Rachel's helpers was Samuel's widowed sister, Sarah Brown, who was living here at the time, between husbands. She had lost two and would shortly marry a third, Richard Hough. Sarah's chief occupation was caring for her own young daughter and for the Bakers' two children: Ann Mary, who was six, and Young Sam, four. They were the first two of a brood that eventually totaled eleven. Meg Rundle, the wife of Yates's lieutenant, did most of the cooking, helped by Molly Bunt. From childhood Molly Bunt had hung around the Bakers at every opportunity; all that they did was strange to her and fascinating. "Molly Bunt" was the white man's version of her Indian name; it was never shortened to a simple "Molly"; no one now knows what the original was. She had almost taken up residence with the Bakers while her band still lived in their town; when they left, she stayed behind and, as far as she could, she stayed as a white woman. Though to Molly Bunt shoes were for Meeting only (she was not a member but she was tolerated), she commonly wore a bodice, petticoats, an apron, and a white cap, like the other women of the household. She understood English quite well and could make shift to speak it, but she spoke as little as possible.

Through winter, spring, and summer, Molly Bunt made herself industriously useful. She could boil soap, dip candles, sweep floors, and wash linen. She did these things willingly if not cheerfully all through winter, spring, and summer. Then, one morning, in mid-October, Molly Bunt would be gone. She would leave her "civilized" clothes hanging on their pegs in the cabin where she slept and, clad in deerskin, with a blanket and some oddments slung on her back from a tumpline across her forehead, she would head north to her own people. This was the hunting season and she needed to be a part of it. Nothing would be seen of her at the ferry house until December; then, as silently as she had gone, she would be back again one morning, taking up her routine without comment where she had left it.

The door of the ferry house had no lock. Travelers arriving after bedtime simply lay down on the kitchen floor and slept. Also, quite often Meg Rundle or Molly Bunt, entering to build up the kitchen fire for breakfast, would find a "walk-about" Indian asleep near

the hearth. Sometimes his squaw and a child or two would be there with him. They were always fed at no charge and, if they seemed to need a little doctoring, Rachel Baker would dose them in whatever way her imagination suggested. Her doses, though unpleasant, never actually poisoned a patient.

Thus Meg was not too startled one January morning to hear the Indian greeting "Netop" from a blanketed figure seated on the hearthstones. She replied cheerfully and went about her work. But Molly Bunt glanced at the stranger and immediately backed out, closing the door behind her. When she returned shortly afterward, she had let down her hair and changed her English garments for her native deerskins. Meg regarded her with round-eyed astonishment. No visitor had ever before had this effect on Molly Bunt. Silently Molly Bunt drew a pot of cider from the cask under the stairs and set it on the hearth in front of the Indian. He added to the puzzle by smiling warmly at Molly Bunt and saying, "Thank thee, daughter," in English.

When Samuel came in for breakfast, the Indian rose, revealing a tall man in his forties wearing buckskin leggings and tunic; his fur matchcoat reached from his shoulders to the ground. He crossed the room to face his host and with the same warm smile said, "Thee is young Baker. I know thy father. I am Tamenend."

"I know thee," said Samuel. "I saw thee here when I was a lad. My father is dead. Sit down with me and eat."

"I hear he is dead. Good man, I liked him. He liked me."

They seated themselves at the table, and as they ate Tamenend explained in a mixture of English and Lenape, with some laconic help from Molly Bunt, that he had been down to Pennsbury to see James Logan, William Penn's Provincial Secretary, and was now on his way north to his own town.

Tamenend was not a Christian, but he had learned his English from Quakers, so he used their pronouns. He was one of the parties to William Penn's original treaty with the Indians. He rated this as the sachem, or

chief, of the Unami, the Turtle clan of the Lenape tribe. Tamenend was the example of all that was best in the Delawares; he was intelligent, generous, and amiable. White men who knew him liked him and respected him. His goodness became so famous among the English that some called him "Saint Tamenend" and named charitable organizations for him. One of these in New York, the Tammany Society, turned later to interests that were less than charitable, but that wasn't Tamenend's fault. He lived until about 1750 and is thought to have been ninety at his death. Nearly seventy years after that, when the ship of the line *State of Delaware* was built, her figurehead was a wooden bust representing Tamenend. At the end of her career the figurehead was set up at the United States Naval Academy, in Annapolis. There it has become a kind of fetish for the midshipmen, who offer it pennies and miscall it "Tecumseh."

Fulling mill

4.

Enterprise

EIGHT miles north of Bakers Ferry and a little more than two miles west of the river there was, and is, a remarkable spring. It keeps its Indian name, Aquetong, said to mean "the place in the pine trees." The enormous flow of the spring, three million gallons a day, is by far the main source of Aquetong Creek, which flows from it to the Delaware. In 1700 Penn granted Richard Heath 1,000 acres in a long narrow tract that included most of the creek. Seven years later Heath built a gristmill along the stream as near its source as he could. In addition to its unfailing volume, Aquetong Creek falls sharply on its way to the river. This made it exceptionally good for turning water wheels; it could furnish enough power for a number of them. In 1712 Philip Williams put up a sawmill of the ancient up-and-down kind, and also a fulling mill. The job of a fulling mill was to finish newly woven woolen cloth by shrinking it and dressing its surface. Part of the shrinking process was beating the cloth in a trough filled with hot water and urine. The plungers that did the beating were powered by a water wheel.

It seems doubtful that Williams tried any dry cleaning here in the woods, but such as was done in these times was usually done by fullers. They covered grease spots with the white clay called fuller's earth, allowed it to dry and absorb at least some of the grease, then brushed it off the cloth. A few men in large centers were beginning to clean woolen clothes with turpentine. This removed the grease all right, but it left behind a smell that lingered for days.

Ichabod Williamson and his son built a rolling and slitting mill on the creek in 1740. They bought forged bar iron, reheated it, and passed it between powered rollers to flatten and lengthen the bars. They then passed the resulting strips, still hot, through opposed disk cutters, mounted on the roller shafts, to produce long nail rods. These were a quarter of an inch square, or smaller. Blacksmiths and "nailers," whose whole business was nail making, pointed them, cut

them to length, and beat the cut ends into large heads.

An oil mill appeared on the creek soon after the rolling mill was built, but the name of the man who started it seems to have been lost. All of the local farmers grew flax and, with great effort and much help from their women, reduced its fibers to linen that could be spun into yarn and woven on the place. Flaxseed was a by-product which the farmers sold to the oil miller. He first crushed the seeds under a water-powered stone wheel that rolled on an iron plate; then he put the resulting mass into mesh bags, woven out of horsehair, and squeezed it in a heavy press. The mesh retained the broken hulls but allowed linseed oil to pass through. The "cake" that was left in the bags made good cattle feed.

John Wells, carpenter, bought half of Richard Heath's land in 1717, and he and his brother-in-law, William Kitchen, settled on it near the mouth of Aquetong Creek. Wells started operating a ferry across the Delaware, probably soon after he arrived, but he didn't get a franchise for it until 1722. Wells also built a gristmill and ran a ferry house. The little settlement that accumulated around it became known as Wells Ferry. In the same year that Wells settled, Richard Heath sold his mill on Aquetong Creek to our old acquaintance Tom Canby. An exception to the four-miles-either-way rule was made in Wells's ferry franchise to permit Tom to have a ferry just below the creek for the use of his family and the customers of his mill. The flow of traffic across the river encouraged a man named Emanuel Coryell to open a ferry house on the New Jersey side and to start a competing ferry.

* * *

The Lenape Indians had agreed that William Penn could have an additional tract of land north of the first one they sold him. Its exact extent had never been determined, but, knowing it eventually would be, people settled on it—Pidcock, Bowman, Heath, and Wells, among them.

As early as 1698 a few settlers pushed in around Scooks Creek, an isolated area twenty-eight miles up the river from Bakers Ferry. Iron ore had been found in the hills there. The pioneers mined it near the surface of the ground and smelted it, a little at a time, in what they called "bloomeries." A bloomery was an open hearth, larger than a blacksmith's forge but similar in principle.

The ironworkers mixed a bushel or so of ore with some crushed limestone and dumped it into the forge along with a lot of charcoal as fuel. By hand pumping a crude bellows, the workers blew up a fire hot enough to reduce the ore to a mushy lump called a "bloom." They hauled their bloom out of the hearth onto a flat stone and beat it with sledgehammers to compact it and to knock out the glassy slag formed by the impurities in the ore combining with the lime from the limestone.

It was a dangerous job. The hammer blows opened pockets of hot liquid slag that flew all over the place and could burn the leather-aproned men severely. Even with reheatings and further hammering, the operation didn't remove all the impurities from the bloom, which, at the end, was reduced to inferior wrought iron. The final hammering probably shaped the mass into a crude bar, bent to a U-shape, that would hang conveniently over the back of a packhorse. The purpose of processing the iron was to sell it; and the only way to get it to a market was on horseback through the woods.

In the early 1720's twelve Philadelphians took up 6,000 acres of land around Scooks Creek and built a blast furnace to smelt iron ore in some quantity. The reason for the large acreage was to supply the enormous quantities of wood needed to make charcoal. Like others of its kind, Durham Furnace, as it was called, was a square, tapering stone tower about twenty feet high. It stood near a high bank, from the top of which a bridge allowed ore, limestone, and charcoal to be brought to the top of the tower in hand carts. Laborers dumped the materials into a more or less egg-shaped chamber, the "bosh," inside the tower where the smelting took place. A simple bellows, but a very large one powered by a water wheel, blew intermittent puffs of air into the bottom of the bosh and made the charcoal burn hot enough to liquefy the iron ore. Being heavy, the iron ran out through a hole in the bottom of the bosh and accumulated in a square, tanklike "hearth" underneath.

Slag floated on the surface of the molten iron in the hearth and the ironworkers skimmed it off with long-handled tools

Bloomery

through holes in a side of the tower. What might be called the front of the tower had a large arched recess in it, deep enough to expose the face of the hearth. The furnace ran without intermission for days on end. Every twelve hours the ironworkers knocked out a clay plug in the hearth face and allowed the liquid iron to flow out into branching ditches which they had hoed in the deep sand floor of the casting arch. There the liquid solidified into brittle pig iron of good quality.

A few years later a forge was added to convert some of the pig iron into "marketable bars" of wrought iron. The process of conversion was similar to what had been done by the bloomery, but the material was more nearly pure and the hammering was done with a 300-pound tilt hammer, powered by a waterwheel. Ichabod Williamson used this bar iron in his rolling mill at Wells Ferry.

*   *   *

It was Robert Durham, the Ironmaster of the Durham Iron Works (it may have been named for him), who solved the problem of getting the iron to market. He took a long look at Lenape dugouts and built a much-enlarged version of them out of planks. The "Durham boats" were double-ended like the dugouts but, unlike them, were flat-bottomed. They were sixty feet long, three and a half feet deep, and only eight feet wide. Men ran them with the current down the river and shot the rapids as they came to them. The "captain" steered in the stern with a sweep thirty-three feet long and the crew fended off the rocks with setting poles. Empty, a Durham boat drew only four inches of water, but a fifteen-ton load of iron ore increased the draft to twenty-eight inches.

A Durham boat could deliver its cargo directly to a buyer in Philadelphia. Below Trenton the boat met tidewater and the crew had to row with four eighteen-foot-long sweeps. They still had help from a strong current when the tide ran out. If they had a fair wind, they could get more help from a small sail on a short mast in the bow. They returned to Trenton by the same means with a cargo of not more than three tons of foodstuffs or merchandise, needed at the furnace or saleable along the upper river. Progress upstream, above Trenton, was extremely slow. The sail was generally useless. Sometimes, on the smooth eddies, the sweeps could be used, but most of the trip had to be made by pole power. Just inside the boat's gunwales, narrow walking boards ran the length of the cargo hold. The men footed these to pole, just as Ben Wilson poled the ferry scow. The rapids reduced upstream progress to a snail's pace, of course, but there is no record of ropes being used to warp the boats through them.

Durham Furnace grew to be one of the three largest ironworks in the American

Durham Furnace and a Durham boat

colonies, so it needed quite a fleet of boats to move its iron. The Durham boat was copied and used by other industries along the river; in fact it was copied for use on other rivers: the Mohawk, the St. Lawrence, and even the Fox River, in Wisconsin. On the Delaware the Durham boats had low crawl-in cabins at both ends in which the crews slept, but they tied up at night to do it. Naturally they preferred to make their stops where there was a ferry house; some nights whole fleets lay over at both Bakers Ferry and Wells Ferry.

The bar

5.

Improvements

AT ABOUT the time that the Durham boats became highly visible on the Delaware, Samuel Baker turned the management of the farm, the ferry, and the ordinary over to his eldest son, Young Sam, who was then in his twenty-fifth year. Aaron and Meg Rundle retired to a cottage on the farm, but their sturdy son, Henry Baker Rundle, known as Henry B., took over the ferryboat, and their daughter, Martha, became chief cook at the ferry house. Samuel Baker, fifty-four, was deeply involved in Provincial and township affairs and was beset with increasing private business interests. Nevertheless, he still kept a quiet eye on the ferry house and enjoyed playing the host there when he could.

Young Sam met the influx of rough-hewn and not always well-behaved rivermen at Bakers Ferry by setting up a bar in the ferry house. It served to guard the stock of liquor from light-fingered patrons. He enclosed a small space in the corner of the big room farthest from the door with a solid wooden barrier almost four feet high. He filled the space between the top of the barrier and the ceiling with a grid of inch-and-a-quarter-thick wooden rods, placed vertically and spaced just over three inches apart. A door half solid and half grille was hinged to a post set against the back wall of the room. A narrow counter topped the solid partition on the fireplace side of the bar. The grid above it was set in a frame hung on hinges, so that it could be raised and hooked up against the ceiling when the bar was open. Shelves under the counter and on the walls back of the bar held pewter mugs and a few wineglasses as well as the limited variety of bottled goods.

A high stand-up desk, made on the place of pine, stood against the wall just outside the bar door. The account book lay on its top, a tall narrow volume bound in sheepskin. Young Sam entered charges in it against local people for food and drink, an occasional bottle of rum, and even passage across the ferry. Accounts were paid twice a year. The arrangement was a practical convenience, because small coins were scarce then and for a long time afterward. Most of the colonies tried to supply the deficiency by issuing paper money in small denominations, but, since few of them could redeem it in hard coin, it was not popular, especially outside the colony that issued it. Pennsylvania put out very little paper, and what it did issue, it backed.

A rack on the wall above the desk held a collection of long clay pipes. When a guest wanted a smoke, he took down a pipe, snapped an inch off the end of its stem for sanitary reasons, and filled it from a tobacco box that stood on the bar. When he did so, he left ha'pence beside the box, or motioned to Young Sam to charge him with the amount. Then he carried his pipe to the hearth and took the smoking tongs from their peg to light it. This involved using the small tongs to lift a coal from the fire and apply it to the tobacco. Some men liked to show off their dexterity by snatching a hot coal onto the pipe with their fingers without being scorched.

Most of the drinks continued to be cider, long enough in the barrel to be a little hard, and Philadelphia ale, bittersweet, with a bit more alcohol in it than beer has. These light drinks were not served across the bar; Willy drew them from casks that stood against the wall near the staircase. Willy was a young Negro, born a slave, whom Samuel Baker had bought and freed. A childhood accident had damaged Willy's left leg so badly that he could not do heavy work, but he performed all sorts of chores around the ferry house to earn his bed and board and a small wage.

Young Sam, or sometimes Henry B., dispensed rum, local whisky, and brandy, neat, over the bar, or came through the gate to mull wine or ale at the fireplace. To do this he added sugar and a little spice to the liquid and then plunged a red-hot loggerhead, often called a flip-dog, into it. A loggerhead looked like a straight poker, but its lower end was thick and usually square. Mulling a drink with it imparted a burnt-leather taste that few people now care for. Once in a while the barman would fill an order for a more elaborate mixed drink: he mulled sweetened ale with a tot of rum in it to make "flip," which he served in an oversize tumbler eight inches high and five inches wide; ale, with molasses and breadcrumbs in it, heated over the fire in a pannikin, made "whistle-belly-vengeance."

* * *

The noise and bustle of the increasing patronage made the ferry house a less than peaceful dwelling and the Baker family was outgrowing the place anyway; so Samuel built himself a new and larger home of stone south of the ferry house but within easy walking distance. Young Sam had a room in the new house and ate enough of his meals there to allow him to discuss farm and ferry business quietly with his father.

* * *

William Penn's first treaty with the In-

Flip glass, clay pipe, loggerhead,
and smoking tongs

dians at Shackamaxon granted him land as far up the Delaware as a man could walk in a day and a half. In 1683 it was measured by the leisurely pace of Penn himself, in the amiable company of several friends and some Indians. A year later Henry Baker erected his house about a mile south of the cedar tree that the expedition picked to mark the northern boundary of the purchase. Penn paid the Indians handsomely and they were content. Later, as has been mentioned,

Meeting House at sunrise on September 19, 1737, three selected athletes walked north on the Durham Road at a furious pace. Wrightstown is about six miles west of Bakers Ferry. The walkers were Edward Marshall, James Yates (the son of Henry Baker's farm manager), and Solomon Jennings, a frontiersman from the Lehigh River. Three mounted surveyors and three Indian witnesses went along. So stiff was the pace that Jennings dropped out after eighteen miles. The other

Samuel Baker's new house

a further agreement extended Penn's land by another day-and-a-half's walk, which was left unmeasured.

Penn died in England in 1718 and two of his sons, John and Thomas, became the proprietors of Pennsylvania. They were lesser men than their father and they lacked his scruples. They saw a chance to make a land grab by exceeding the intention of the second agreement and they seized it. Secretly, they sent Joseph Doan with some other men to find the most advantageous route for a walk and to mark it by blazes on trees.

Starting from the Wrightstown Friends

two pressed on perhaps fifteen miles farther and quit for the night just beyond the Blue Mountains. The Indians quit, too, in disgust at the obvious cheat.

Marshall and Yates made a late start in the rain the next morning with some new Indians, who gave up after ten miles. Yates soon reached the end of his endurance, but Marshall pushed on to Pocono Mountain. He had covered something like four times the distance Penn made on the first walk. The surveyors at once ran a line to the Delaware River, but they cheated, too. To include as much land as possible, their line took a

33

northeasterly direction, instead of the honest easterly one that would have been a right angle to the path of the walk. Edward Marshall had acquired 750,000 acres of land for the Penn brothers, but the effort was too much for him; he died the next day.

The Lenape never forgave the swindle, and when war came, in 1750, they took the side of the French against the English. The Quakers, too, were disgusted, but the new German and Scotch-Irish settlers, who were pouring into Pennsylvania, were less particular. They started filling up the new land immediately.

* * *

At about ten o'clock on a gray morning, not long after the Indian Walk, Henry B. Rundle came to the Baker house and found the family at breakfast. He walked into the room and spoke without ceremony: "We have a poser at the ferry. A man with a wain and a pair of horses is on the other shore seeking to cross. The scow will carry his wagon or his horses, but not both. It's too short."

"I see. Does thee know who the man is?"

"Yes. I rowed the bateau over and talked to him. He is Robert Clayton from Prince Town. He has a load of rags for the paper mill on Wissahickon Creek. His way is through Newtown. He'll come back this way, he says, with whatever load he can pick up."

"I know him," said Young Sam. "We should try to get him over. I'll come with thee and we'll see what can be done about it."

"Finish thy breakfast, he can wait."

"No. I've had enough. If we bring the horses over first, Clayton will have no way to get his wagon on the scow, so we must bring the wain over first," said Sam as they walked toward the landing. "Have Clayton *back* his wain onto the scow, unhitch his horses, and stay with them while thee ferries the wain over. I'll find a way to get it off on this side."

Henry B. did as he was told without comment. The rags made a light load and Clayton turned his vehicle around and backed it aboard with no difficulty. Across the river Henry B. found Young Sam and Amos Chew waiting with a span of oxen and a long log chain. With one end of the chain hitched to the ox yoke and the other to the rear axle of the wain, and with Henry B. steering the tongue, the team easily pulled the wagon backward off the ferryboat—even though they had to climb up the slope of the bank

34

to do it. Once ashore, Amos swung his animals downhill, turned the wain with Henry B.'s help, and pulled it—still backward—up the gentler slope of the lane to the fairly level stretch in front of the ferry house. It was after one o'clock when Clayton mounted his near-side horse to take off for Newtown.

"How y' goin' t'git me back across?" he asked.

"Thee'll drive thy wain to the landing and unhitch. Henry B. will carry thee and thy horses over and bring the ferry back. Then we will muster what men we can and push the wain on the scow. All thee'll have to do is hitch thy horses to it and draw it off."

"That oughta do it," said Robert. "Giddup!"

"Yep, it ought to do it," said Henry B., "but we can't use half a day and all the men on the place to get many wagons across the river!"

"Thee's right, Henry B. We need a longer scow," said Young Sam. "There will be more wagons and some will have four horses to them. The men can build a new boat during this winter."

"It'll take two men to pole four horses and a wagon," Henry B. said.

The new ferry, forty feet long and tarred on the outside, went into service in the spring of 1738. It was a flatboat, like the one it replaced. The most obvious difference was in the gangplanks at the ends. They projected farther than the old ones, and instead of being turned inboard to lie on the deck, they were merely raised high enough to clear the water. Stout poles fixed across the ends of the gangplanks served as levers to raise them. It took two men to depress the ends of the poles and secure them with loops of rope that were attached to the deck for the purpose.

Instead of the ring that served to bridle the old ferry to its cross-river rope, the new boat was held on its course by two pulleys that rolled on the rope. Lines from each pulley were made fast to cleats at each end of the craft. At the start of a crossing the ferryman shortened the forward line and lengthened the after one. This placed the ferryboat at an angle to the current and made the flow of the river help in pushing it across in much the same way that wind acts on a sail.

On the day of the ferry's launch, Young Sam posted new rates. He wrote them with a quill pen, framed them in a small box with a glass door, and fastened the box beside the ferry house door. The list went like this:

Tolls for the Ferry
*One foot passenger, 3d.**
Three or more, 1d. each
Horse and rider, 6d.
Two or more, 4d. each
One ox, 8d.
Two or more, 6d. each
Sheep, 1d. each
Hogs, 3d. each
Chair or cart, one horse and driver, 1s. 6d.
Four-wheeled carriage, two horses and
  driver, 3s.
Wain, two horses and driver, 2s. 6d.
Wagon, four horses and driver, 4s.
All rates are double after nine at night

* * *

* In the first half of the twentieth century, an English penny—1d., for *denarius*—was worth approximately two American cents. Its value in the eighteenth century, based upon what it would buy, was much greater than that, but it is hard to say exactly how much greater. American laborers at that time got a shilling (1s.) a day—that is, twelve pence—and could survive on it.

Among the first passengers on the new ferry was one who got a special rate and whose tolls were entered in the account book. He made a round trip every week—over on Tuesday, back on Friday. He was the post rider, a wizened elderly man known as "Horse," though his name was actually Horace. Nobody knew his last name, which was Smith. His route ran between Philadelphia and New Brunswick, New Jersey. His mail traveled in two leather pouches slung behind the saddle across the back of his languorous nag. One pouch held letters for people along his route; the other was for through mail with addresses as far north as Boston, or going the other way, as far south as Charleston, though most such long-distance mail traveled by sea. Horse turned over what he carried of this through mail to the postmasters at the ends of his route; they sent it on by other riders. The Philadelphia postmaster was Benjamin Franklin. Even in summer when the roads were dry a letter took three weeks to get from Philadelphia to Boston.

If Horse had mail for anyone within about five miles of Baker's, he left it at the ferry house to be picked up and paid for by the person to whom it was addressed. Sometimes a letter lay on top of the high desk for three months before it was delivered. Such letters were directed accordingly: "For Thomas Hudson, to be left at Samuel Baker's ordinary." The postmaster at the point of origin marked the amount of the postage (a single sheet, one shilling) above the address and scrawled his signature. Mail originating at either end of Horse's route was recorded there and he had to turn in the postage he collected for it; but when he picked up a local letter for delivery farther along the way, he was on his own and the postage went into his long purse. Horse also picked up some profit by carrying small packages and doing errands along the way—he once led a cow to Newtown for Samuel Baker. Occasionally a traveler, especially a woman journeying alone, would deliberately seek Horse's company, but on most trips his way was lonely. His steed knew the road and ambled along it half asleep; Horse passed the time knitting stockings and mittens, which he sold by the wayside to whoever would buy.

When Horse announced his arrival at the

"Horse" the postrider

ferry house on Tuesdays with a blast on his tin horn, the proprietor himself usually came out to meet him; so did anyone else who was in the place at the time. Samuel made a point of being there because, with the mail, the post rider delivered the latest edition of *The Pennsylvania Gazette,* only four days old. After Samuel had read the foreign and local news, the long flowery essays by gentlemen who hid their identities under assumed classical names, and all the advertisements for runaway servants and cows, the paper was left in the public room to be passed from hand to hand for the information of all comers. Articles of prime interest were often read aloud and earnestly discussed. So great was the demand for the sheet that Young Sam had to post a small notice saying: "Friends learning to read will please use last week's *Gazette.*"

the Swan

6.

Expansion

WHETHER or not the ease of getting back and forth across the ferry had anything to do with it isn't recorded, but in 1742 Young Sam married a New Jersey girl, Elizabeth Burroughs. Sam was thirty-two years old when he married, and he had already served as a Commissioner for Bucks County and as Coroner. It was unusual in these times for a man to stay single so long.

The new boat at Bakers Ferry was built none too soon. Philadelphia had grown and was still growing fast. It had long passed the time when the land in its immediate neighborhood could supply it with food and firewood. It now drew upon the surrounding counties, and on the western part of New Jersey. Part of what came from the neighboring colony crossed the Delaware on Baker's ferry. The Bucks County township opened new roads, and straightened old ones somewhat and cleared trees from the rights of way. The surfaces were left to nature except in low spots, where logs placed side by side across the route made "corduroy roads" over bogs. None of these roads were wider than

what would now be called a lane; and their ruts, holes, and bumps far outdid anything describable as rough.

The most practical vehicle for such surfaces was a cart with two very large and strong wheels that would "bridge" the inequalities. The chaise, or "chair," as people more often called it, was built this way and hence was the most useful and popular private carriage. It could be pulled by one strong athletic horse. A big ox cart was good for hauling cargo on these roads, but its capacity was limited; only a wagon could carry a really large load. Country blacksmiths and a few specialist wheelwrights built stout wagons that would fill the bill. Since all the wrights were Englishmen, it is possible that some of them built replicas of the ponderous English "stage wagons," which had wheels eight inches wide and bodies with flared sides and ends. In England these hauled huge loads over roads little smoother than American roads, but it took eight horses to pull one of them—and it never had to cross a ferry. This made the behemoths impractical here, so the wheelwrights turned to lighter vehicles carrying smaller loads that two horses could pull in dry weather.

Such a wagon was useful on farms as well as for overland hauling. It had a box body about nine feet long and three and a half feet wide with a couple of full-length slats along each side, supported on brackets, to allow a light load, like hay, to extend over the wheels. These wheels stood five feet high in the rear, but the front ones were smaller to allow the vehicle to make sharper turns. Leaning outward, as wooden wheels must, they had to be coned to allow their wide tires to roll true on the ground. "Coned" means that the diameter of the outer face was smaller than that of the inner face. Wheelwrights had not yet learned how to shrink a continuous iron tire onto a wheel. Instead they nailed on short sections, called strakes.

The increasing number of wagoners made new patrons for the ferry house and, with the rivermen, sometimes strained its capacity. When a stage line between Philadelphia and New Brunswick started using Baker's ferry twice a week, Young Sam and his father considered ways to enlarge the place.

The first stages were simply two-horse wagons carrying perhaps five passengers and a driver. Dr. Alexander Hamilton (no kin of the later statesman) described them as "light convenient wagons, built somewhat chaise fashion." His description suggests the so-called "pleasure wagon" widely used by farmers to convey the family to church or to haul light loads. How the word "pleasure" applied is difficult to see. The vehicle was springless and had no top of any kind to keep off the weather. "Somewhat chaise fashion" suggests that these particular pleasure wagons may have had tops, since chaises did have them.

Within a few years, traffic increased so much that a larger and stronger vehicle was needed. Perhaps the earlier, light rig was called a "stage wagon"; this heavier one certainly was. The word "stage," in this sense, did not describe the wagon itself; it denoted that the vehicle made its journey by stages, stopping at certain points for the convenience of passengers and to replace tired horses with fresh ones.

The Yankee stage wagons were altogether different from the English ones—even in purpose—and different from an ordinary American wagon, too. They were lighter and shorter, but they remained wagons; they had no springs at all. Ten passengers and a

One-horse chaise

Early two-horse stage wagon (conjectural)

driver sat in a stage wagon on bare boards, three passengers to a board and one up front with the driver. The high, sloping tailgate gave the three on the rear seat some support for their backs; the rest got none. For this reason, women sat in the rear, but they had to enter at the front and climb over the other boards to get to their seats. A fixed top, covered with tarred canvas, kept sun and rain off the riders and roll-down curtains of the same stuff gave them further protection in really bad weather. The occupants of the two ends of a board could hang on to the stanchions that supported the top and thus spare themselves a little of the pain of rocking and bumping. The middle passenger could only clutch the edge of the board he sat on, or, in real trouble, grab a seatmate on one side or the other.

The bulkier luggage, covered by a tarpaulin, rode on a rack that was attached to the rear of the wagon. Small stuff could be stowed under the benches inside. The familiar shapes of modern hand luggage were not to be seen; even the now-vanished carpetbag had not yet been invented. A traveler carried toilet articles and other small matters in a "poke," a small cloth bag closed by a drawstring. Hatboxes, or the somewhat smaller bandboxes (made originally for holding men's neckwear), could serve the same purpose. Both kinds were made of pasteboard,

or of very thin wood, and were usually covered with decorated paper. Some people carried extra clothing in a simple bundle, but garments were more often folded into a strip of canvas which was then rolled and secured with straps or ropes. The contraption was spoken of as a valise, or a portmanteau. A more elegant portmanteau served the affluent, but it must have been an awkward thing to pack. It was a cowhide cylinder, about two and a half feet long and eight inches in diameter, split lengthwise into two halves hinged together. Straps around its ends kept it closed and a handle was provided on the middle of the upper half. Travelers also used small trunks, or "boxes," some made of sole leather but most of them of wood covered with deerhide—with the hair left on. Such a trunk had an arched top, iron handles at both ends, and a capacity of less than two cubic feet.

Travelers bound for New York changed to another stage line at New Brunswick—and might have to wait a day or two at a tavern until their vehicle was ready to leave. This second stage deposited them at Perth Amboy, where they transferred to a sailing ferry for Manhattan. Southbound travelers had a choice of routes: They could go from Philadelphia to Newcastle, Delaware, by boat, take a stage across the peninsula to the head of the Elk River, and then another boat down

the Chesapeake Bay to Annapolis; or they could take a through stage line from Philadelphia to Annapolis, using a ferry across the Susquehanna River to Havre de Grace. This ferry seems to have been unique in the colonies. A continuous rope, attached to both ends of the boat, passed around a pulley on one shore and around a capstan on the other. Two horses, blindfolded to keep them from becoming dizzy, walked in a circle around the capstan to turn it and so pull the ferry back and forth.

A northbound stage wagon left Philadelphia at 3:00 A.M. on Tuesdays and reached New Brunswick, roughly sixty miles away by road, between 8:00 and 9:00 that night—in good weather. Four horses pulled it, and the whole outfit crossed the Delaware at one trip on Baker's ferry. Every fifteen miles or so the team was replaced by fresh horses. An extra pair was stabled at the foot of each of the two steep hills on the route. These, added to the front of the team, in the charge of a postilion who rode one of them, helped in pulling the load up the grade. Even so,

able-bodied passengers had to get out and walk up the hills in very bad weather. The stage wagon had no brakes—an American novelty yet to be invented—and the two wheel horses, "sitting" back against their breechings, were not strong enough to hold it back going down one of these hills. Therefore the driver had to stop at the top and chain the rear wheels to the undercarriage so that they couldn't turn but slid like runners down the slope. Freight wagon drivers didn't bother with chains. When they came to a declivity, they cut a stout sapling at the roadside and thrust it through the spokes of both rear wheels. The sapling caught against the undercarriage and kept the wheels from turning.

Changing the stage wagon team took ten minutes or less (in later coaching days it was done in one minute flat), but at two of the stops the stage lay over long enough for the passengers to eat a hasty meal. The Baker's ferry house was a horse-changing station, and the dinner stop in both directions. The dinners, substantial, because these

people had been traveling for more than seven hours, put a strain on the kitchen. The food had to be hot and ready to eat at once, and no one could tell exactly when the stage would get there. The driver blew a horn to announce his arrival, but that gave not more than three minutes' warning on the northern trip. The southern trip was better. Willy, on watch, could see the stage embarking on the ferry and even make shift to count its passengers. There might be eleven to feed—or only one, the driver.

Winter weather made stage wagon travel hazardous and sometimes stopped it entirely. Ice in the Delaware prevented the operation of the ferry for some days every year, both when it froze from shore to shore and when thaws brought great chunks of floating ice down the stream. Thick ice might bear the weight of a wagon and allow it to cross without the aid of the ferry, but this happened so rarely that it was a tale told by old men to prove that "winters ain't like they used to be." Freshets, too, when they raised the water almost to the doorstep of the ferry house,

forced immediate action to keep the ferry-boat from being washed away, and no one thought of trying to cross. The Durham boats headed downstream to Philadelphia could ride the crest of a freshet at high speed, but the crews then had to wait over there until the river dropped to normal before they could return upstream.

Aside from the difficulty of getting across the river, cold weather made trouble for the stage wagons on the roads. Bad enough in summer, these became horrible in the winter. Simple freezing hardened the ruts so that the jolting of the vehicle, miserable at best, became almost insupportable. Thaws created morasses of mud into which wheels sank to the hubs. Drifted snow increased the difficulty of pulling the wagon and at the same time caused the horses to flounder and plunge, which cut down their pulling power. East of the Hudson River winter traffic took to runners, but here a warm spell was likely to leave a sleigh marooned. Frequently the stage wagon upset, and all male passengers had to lend their strength to putting it back

43

on its wheels. Once in a while the outfit became hopelessly stuck. When that happened, the driver, to keep his passengers alive, built a roadside fire with flint-and-steel and damp wood—no small job. Then he mounted one of the horses and rode ahead or back to get help. The Bakers were sometimes called upon to send extra horses or, if the stage were damaged, a farm wagon to bring in the passengers. This meant that they were stuck at the ferry house for several days, and it might be necessary to slaughter a pig, or a sheep, to feed them. The public was aware of such hazards and, whenever possible, arranged to do its traveling in warm weather, beset by nothing worse than dust and insects.

Local people planning to travel one way or the other met the stage at the ferry and bought a seat from the driver, if one was available. If none was, they had either to try again next week or to hire a horse, or a horse and chair, from Young Sam. The problem seldom arose because nearly everyone in the vicinity of Bakers Ferry owned at least one horse.

Colonial stage wagon passengers didn't have to worry about highwaymen. In England a traveler commonly carried what money he would need for his journey in clinking gold coin. Thus the "take" from a coachload of passengers could be a considerable sum, all of it completely negotiable. Travelers went in constant and justified fear of the masked horseman brandishing a huge pistol who would bid them "stand and deliver." An armed guard frequently rode on the box with the coachman. He carried a brass blunderbuss, loaded with scrap iron, but he seems seldom to have been effectual.

Many of the highwaymen were hanged; others were "transported" to the colonies, but the colonies had little to fear from them. Pirates on the sea, yes, but highwaymen on the roads, no. This was due partly to the opportunities for honest profit that felons found here and partly to the unprofitable nature of colonial travelers. Americans had little of anything that would clink. They carried letters of credit, drafts on merchants, or, if they were Southerners, tobacco warehouse receipts. To anyone but the person to whom these things were issued, they were worthless paper.

* * *

The farm stable stood some distance from the ferry house, so the Bakers built a new

one nearby to shelter the stage horses and those of travelers who stopped for the night. No space was needed for hay storage, so what would normally have been the loft served as a dormitory for freight wagon men. Small windows let in some light, and a narrow stair, running up the outside wall, provided an entrance. The men rolled in their own blankets on straw mattresses placed on the floor.

With the stable built, Samuel and Young Sam turned their attention to the ferry house. The increase of patronage crowded the public room only occasionally, but it took less than a crowd to interfere with cooking around the fireplace, and the cooks got in the way of the patrons. A new kitchen on the river end of the house was the obvious solution, and it might as well be two stories high and permit four bedrooms on its second floor. To achieve this, the addition, built of stone plastered over with stucco, was made rather larger than its use as a kitchen required. Even so, the bedrooms were cubbyholes. The two at the head of the narrow twisting stair were especially small and the other two were only a little larger. All four were unheated except for a faint warmth from the chimneys. On cold nights Willy warmed the beds with a brass warming pan. Each room had one small window and each was entered from a little hall that was totally dark when all the doors were shut. Two of the rooms had double beds in them, but the stairwell and the old keeping room chimney cut so deeply into the front rooms next to the old building that they could hold only cots which left the occupants little more than enough room to turn around.

The idea of leveling land occurred to no one, so, because of the slope toward the river, the floors of the new addition lay about fifteen inches lower than those of the old house. This forced Willy and Molly Bunt to carry all food up two steps from the kitchen to the taproom, as the old keeping room–kitchen came now to be called. However, the

Clock jack

same difference of levels shortened, by two risers, the stairs that led from beside the taproom fireplace to the new sleeping quarters.

Cooking arrangements in the new kitchen remained the same as those in the old one except that there was now an iron crane to hold pots over the fire, and the new oven door now faced the room from the breast of the chimney, instead of opening awkwardly in the side wall of the fireplace. There was also a better system for roasting meat. Instead of the old hand-turned spit there was a clock jack that slowly and steadily rotated the roast hanging from it without also roasting a human face. The spring and works of this machine were enclosed in a cylindrical brass case. A ring at the top allowed it to be hung on a big nail driven into the manteltree. A brass rod with a hook on its lower end projected from the bottom of the case. Inside the case a strong spring, restrained by a train of gears, provided power to rotate the hook. The cook wound the spring with a small crank which she hung on the nail between windings.

The new kitchen made life easier for the cooks and other servants. They had plenty of space for work tables and for storing utensils and dishes. Though pewter remained the material of most of the plates and bowls and all of the large chargers, some pottery put

45

in its appearance. A potter at Dolington, only two miles away, made shiny red pitchers, jugs, and mugs that were serviceable and quite handsome. Iron knives and iron two-tined forks, both with wooden handles, now appeared on the ferry house table, though the knives got far more use than the forks. The bar stuck to pewter mugs and "cans," which could be dented and bent but not easily broken. When Young Sam made punch with rum, sugar, hot water, and lemon juice (lemon juice came in bottles from Spain), he served it in bowls.

The kitchen had its own door to the outside and Sam had a well dug near it to remove the need of trips to the river for water. The well had to be only fifteen feet deep. The three windows of the kitchen and the four of the rooms overhead had "modern" wooden sashes in them. Their lower section could be raised for ventilation, but they had no cords-and-weights; they had to be propped open with sticks. The carpenters made the entire sash by hand on the spot. No putty held the panes of glass in the sash. Instead, rabbets held the glass not only on the inner side, as in a modern sash, but on the outside also, where points and putty are now used. The frame was made in two parts, front and back, to accomplish this. Replacing a broken

pane required taking the frame apart by removing the dowels at its corners.

The rough shakes that roofed the main building showed their more than fifty years of service, so the Bakers had them replaced with shingles like those on the new addition. The carpenters nailed them on the roof, but Sam bought them ready to use from two brothers on Jericho Mountain (really a hill) who made shingles for a living—splitting them from billets with frows and then tapering and smoothing them with drawknives.

When they had finished the new wing and the roofs, the carpenters went on to further improvements in the main building. Using the same kind of dark central hall that served the kitchen wing, they partitioned the large space over the taproom into six small unheated bedrooms (eight pence a night). Henry Baker's large bedroom remained unchanged for the use of special guests (a shilling and sixpence). Sam refurnished the old parlour under this room as a kind of private dining room–lounge for the shilling-and-sixpence guests. Windows had to be cut for the new rooms, so Sam had all the old leaded casements replaced with wooden sash and added solid paneled shutters to make the front look, as he put it, "seemly." For the same reason, he dressed up the old entrance with a small wooden stoop and a shingled canopy over it. Finally, he painted the clapboards white and the shutters and doors very dark green. No record of a sign survives, but almost certainly the tavern had one.

The older Samuel, now in his late sixties, had some fifteen years of life ahead of him, but he thought of himself as an old man and behaved accordingly. His pace was slow and he carried a crutch-topped cane on which he was never seen to depend for help. For reasons that are not clear, he had long since deeded the ferry, the ferry house, and six hundred acres of the farm to Young Sam and had apparently sold the rest of his land, except for the small homestead tract south of

The rebuilt ferry house

the ferry. He became less and less interested in business and devoted himself to contemplation, conversation, and amiable criticism of the world around him. In his retirement he was almost daily at the tavern, as we may now call it, though it remained "the ferry house" to the neighborhood. His interest in the place had become largely social; Young Sam discussed business with him but usually acted upon his own decisions.

Though Samuel Baker was a kind and genial man, he was, like his father before him, conscious of occupying a superior social position. His son, however, gave no thought to precedence. Tall, physically powerful, soft-spoken, and friendly, he belonged to his community; he thought himself no better than his neighbors and thought them no better than he. He remained a devout Quaker but did not feel the same need to assert his beliefs that his father felt and his

grandfather, particularly, had felt. Though he felt uneasy about Jews and Roman Catholics, Sam could meet an Anglican, now often called an "Old Lighter," or a "New Lighter" or even a Baptist as a fellow Christian and treat him accordingly. A New Lighter was one in whom a religious fervor had been aroused by the evangelism of the famous preacher George Whitefield, who had traveled through the colonies. His converts were very vocal about their new convictions.

Quite unconsciously, Sam expressed his simple outlook in the clothes he wore, which, of course, also reflected the passage of time. His go-to-Meeting coat was of brown homespun wool with pewter buttons that he fastened only in cold weather. Ordinarily it hung open and exposed a vest of the same material that reached halfway to his knees. At home, in the modest house that he and Elizabeth occupied and at the ferry house, he

47

habitually wore the vest without the coat. On First Day his breeches were tan kersey; on weekdays, leather. Philadelphia was becoming known through the middle colonies for the manufacture of deerskin breeches—the first ready-made garments in America. Sam's stockings were nearly always knitted wool, worn in boots most days but in shoes, fastened with square silver buckles, for Meeting. He wore his hair long, but he "clubbed" it with a narrow black ribbon at the back of his neck.

Sam's mother, Rachel, changed no part of her habitual dress in her long lifetime, but her daughter-in-law, Elizabeth, advanced a little with the changing style. She wore a sack dress of which the bodice and sleeves were made as integral parts. The overskirt hung from the top of the bodice all the way to her heels in back, but it did not trail on the ground like that of a worldly lady. It was fastened to the bottom of the bodice and its two halves did not meet in front but hung open all the way down to reveal a narrow panel of petticoat. Her best dress was gray,

Lady wearing a farthingale

with a lighter gray petticoat that was quilted in a simple lozenge pattern. More elegant petticoats were quilted with flower patterns and swirling leaves. Elizabeth didn't wear a farthingale. A farthingale was two half-dome-shaped frames of whalebone, fastened to a belt, a contraption that great ladies wore to extend their dresses on both sides. Elizabeth wore a plain white cap at all times. Two lappets hung from its corners as streamers. Hers was a modest "plain" dress for the times, but in Meeting some elderly eyebrows were lifted at it.

Young Sam and Elizabeth

Bull's Head

7.

Taverns in Country and Town

UP THE river at Wells Ferry a complicated series of marriages, widowings, and inheritances had, by 1760, brought the ferry houses on both sides of the river, and both Wells's ferryboat and the competing New Jersey ferryboat, into the hands of John Coryell, Emanuel's son. The hamlet on the Pennsylvania shore then became known as Coryells Ferry. The ferry house there became Coryell's Tavern. It was no bigger or more important than the Bakers' establishment, but John ran it well. He was a genial, intelligent man and, when the time came to take sides, he was a staunch patriot and, incidentally, a personal friend of General George Washington.

Not only did many of the iron-laden Durham boats lay over at Coryells Ferry, but other Durham boats were loaded there with barrels of flour and of corn meal, barrels of linseed oil, and bundles of iron nail rods and of flattened iron bars for the use of blacksmiths. Local farmers brought their products to the landing for shipment; wheat, salt meat, live pigs and sheep, and crates of chickens went down the river to Philadelphia.

Freight wagons and stage wagons crossed the river on Coryell's ferry as they did on Baker's. By the time Coryell took over, some of the wagons from western Pennsylvania were Conestogas, and Coryell built a new ferryboat, sixty feet long, to carry them. The German farmers in Lancaster County had devised these wagons to carry large loads long distances over the roughest of roads. Their tall wheels were very strong and their big bodies curved upward toward both ends like New England fishing dories. The high sides and ends of the bodies sloped outward to increase capacity and to concentrate the weight of the load on the floor. Arched wooden bows supported hand-woven tow-linen covers that kept the weather off the cargo. Since the bows grew gradually taller toward both ends, and since the end bows slanted forward and backward, the shape of the cover emphasized the fore-and-aft curve of the body. These wagons had another novel feature: they had brakes, though setting

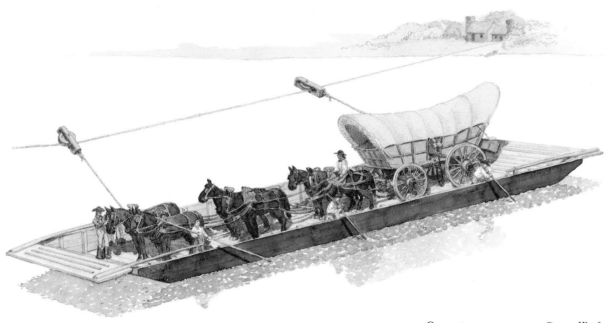

Conestoga wagon on Coryell's ferry

them required a brakeman who rode on a board projecting from the side of the wagon and pulled on a long brake handle at need. The driver rode a saddle on the near wheeler and controlled the six big horses with a single jerk line, a "blacksnake" whip, and a vocabulary of strong language. The Conestoga wagons were copied even more widely than the Durham boats. They hauled freight all through the colonies and, as "Pittsburg" wagons, eventually reached the western plains, though they proved too heavy to last there.

* * *

Everywhere north of the Patapsco River, and almost as far west as settlement reached, the countryside was dotted with taverns and ordinaries. Most of them were even simpler than Baker's or Coryell's; many, simple to the point of crudity, were revolting. Food in them was likely to be cornmeal mush and something, or simply mush and nothing. Beds were at best hard wooden platforms, with ticking bags filled with straw, corn husks, or dried leaves as mattresses. Of blankets, the less said the better. Even these beds were in short supply and complete

strangers commonly found themselves in bed together. They seldom found themselves alone there. Fleas and other small creatures made their homes in the mattresses and dined upon the occupants. Those guests who were so eccentric as to wash before breakfast (mush) had to go outside to the pump to do it.

The better country taverns usually were located strategically at a ferry or at a busy crossroads. A very few were such pleasant places that people spoke of their excellence and travelers deliberately planned to break their journeys at them; some even detoured to reach them. The best of all rural hostelries was the "Sun Inn" at Bethlehem, Pennsylvania. It appears to have been the only colonial tavern that was formally called an inn. The good Moravian Brothers ran it the way they did everything—as well as possible. The "Sun" provided excellent food, offered handsomely furnished suites as well as individual rooms, and detailed a personal servant to each guest in the more expensive accommodations.

South of the Potomac, the plantation owners hungered so much for contact with the world that they welcomed all travelers, even to the point of posting servants at their gates to invite all passersby to stop. Since wayfarers could be sure of free entertainment, its character varying with their social standing, there was not enough business to support taverns in the open country. But a county seat had at least an ordinary, which hummed with life for a short time while court was sitting and slumbered the rest of the year. The same thing happened on a larger scale in the Provincial capitals, like Williamsburg and Annapolis. Each had a number of taverns and ordinaries, some good, which did most of their business in a few weeks, while the Provincial assemblies and the high courts were in session. Along with others less pretentious, the "Raleigh Tavern" at Williamsburg has been restored to its handsome original condition.

Few country taverns approached the grandeur of the "Sun" and the "Raleigh." Most of them started life as private dwellings, the way the Bakers' did, and had additions built onto them when need arose. A landlord whose hostelry was actually built for its purpose usually boasted of the fact. Many country tavern keepers, especially on the western fringes of settlement, also "kept store," perhaps in a lean-to at one end of their building. Everywhere the local tavern was the local center, serving as club, bar, restaurant, dance hall, courthouse, and even jail. Probably no dance was ever held at the Bakers' ferry house. The Quakers didn't approve of dancing, nor did the Puritans in New England; but in the rest of the colonies the taverns rocked on Saturday nights as the local boys and girls footed "country dances" (*contre danses*), which we call square dances, to "Old Dan Tucker" and "Turkey in the Straw" scraped off a fiddle.

Ordinaries along important roads catered to the "waggoners" who hauled freight over long distances with six-horse Conestoga rigs. This meant providing a yard for parking wagons, a stable to shelter horses, and a large room with a fire where the men could eat and sleep. It also meant serving great quantities of solid food at low prices.

The Sun Inn

The Raleigh Tavern

Quite often taverns that served the "carriage trade" also entertained wagoners in what amounted to separate establishments, even though they were housed in the same building. Such places usually made a further separation between the quarters for resident guests and the bar, with a separate entrance for each. When you see, in the eastern United States, an old house with two doors facing the road, you may be almost certain that it started life as a tavern.

Wherever settlement was sufficiently organized to take the law out of the hands of a posse of neighbors and put it into the hands of a court, the list of selected jurors, tacked on the tavern door, was considered sufficient notice of service. If the designated juror didn't see the list himself, a crony would see it and would report the summons. In all the colonies, local magistrates and justices of the peace commonly heard cases in tavern taprooms, as Henry Baker had. In some colonies, especially those of New England, circuit-riding judges held formal jury trials in taverns. When a criminal trial was on the docket, the accused was often locked in an upstairs tavern room overnight, preferably an attic room because escape from it was harder than from a lower one. The tavern keeper was paid by the county for housing the prisoner and for feeding the jury their breakfasts and dinners.

As a natural convenience, stocks, a pillory, and a whipping post often stood in a tavern yard. Along with goods, animals, land, and slaves, paupers and convicted criminals were auctioned at vendues in the yard. The paupers were sometimes old and the county would pay something to the purchaser for their keep; more often they were children, and in spite of some abuses, their purchaser usually bought them out of human kindness and they became as much his children as his own offspring. There being no "gaols" outside of those in large towns, country criminals were condemned to labor for terms of months or years and farmers bid against one another for the benefit of the labor.

New England townships, from early times, were governed by town meetings normally held in the Meeting House—that is, the church. Meeting Houses were unheated. Although it was good for the soul to shiver while praying, there was no real need for self-punishment while transacting business. So, in cold weather, the meetings usually adjourned across the Common to the tavern.

Muster Day, held once or twice a year and sometimes oftener, was usually profitable to the landlord of the principal tavern in a township. Quite often he was the captain of the local militia company and just as often he was accused (in his absence) of calling frequent musters to get the business they brought him. Musters were almost always held on Saturdays. Through much of the day the files practiced close-order drill and the manual of arms, with fairly frequent rest periods for visits to the bar. Officers were expected to treat the men under them to at least one round of rum. There is a story of a New Jersey company being marched through a taproom in a prepared maneuver that gave every man a noggin, without breaking step, and had them all back on the drill field in ten minutes. A long break was called for dinner at the expense of the taxpayers. Sometimes there was more drill after dinner; more often those who could still navigate engaged in horse races, foot races, wrestling matches, and other athletic contests, not excluding informal fist fights.

Even without the militia, enterprising tavern keepers promoted various contests, races both foot and horse, and games, to attract customers on holidays. Logget was one such game. It was played like quoits except that there were no "ringers." The iron horseshoes needed for them were too valuable for frivolous use, so the players pitched short billets of wood at the pegs instead. Turkey shoots were popular. The modern versions of these contests award turkeys (ready-dressed) to the highest scorers firing at targets or clay pigeons; the colonials shot at live turkeys. Men with muskets shot from 110 yards; rifle-

Dance at a country tavern

Muster Day

men, from 160 yards. This would have been a bonanza for the long rifle of a frontiersman from the mountains. Out there the customary mark for a shooting match was a nail driven into a tree at 200 yards, and many a man could hit the nail on the head. Of course handmade nails had heads half an inch wide.

In early days, and on the frontier much later, a bush, or an empty jug, hung in front of a house was sufficient notice that liquor was sold inside. From the middle of the eighteenth century most taverns had names and displayed them painted on wooden signs, along with an appropriate design that would be recognizable to those who could not read. Just to be sure, the taverns often hung up a bush, too. In some colonies the sign was an indication that the premises were licensed; if the license lapsed, the sheriff took the sign down.

In England, where such things were familiar, many inn signs showed designs taken from heraldry, and even the illiterate would recognize a griffon on the sign of a hostelry

called "The Ballard Arms," or simply "The Griffon." To Americans a griffon would be only a crazy-looking mixed-up lion with wings and a beak. A number of English inns had strange "quaint" names. It's said that most of these were due to errors on the part of sign painters and the boniface made do with what he got. Thus one who wished to name his house "God Encompasseth Us" got "Goat and Compasses," and the exuberant landlord who wanted "Bacchanals" got "Bag o' Nails," both with corresponding pictures.

Americans needed something simple and familiar. This nearly ruled out heraldry; almost the only use of it was the crossed keys of the papal arms, also used by the archbishops of York. Anyone could recognize two crossed keys. There must have been at least fifty taverns in the colonies called "Cross Keys." Some colonial signs assumed with reason that the public could read, and displayed only the owner's name and something like "Lodging for Man and Beast," but most bore the name of some familiar object: "The Plough," "The Horse and Wagon," "The

54

Wheat Sheaf," "The Anchor," "The Green Tree," "The White Horse." These were all in Bucks County. "The Anchor," well named because it served frequently as a reference point, was only a little way west of Bakers Ferry.

Tavern keepers were licensed by the Provincial assemblies, which looked carefully into the personal histories of applicants and tried to pick only those of high principles and reasonable sobriety. New England landlords seem to have accepted the job as a public duty rather than as an opportunity and apparently felt that they conferred a favor on the traveler by allowing him to pay for shelter and food. Tavern keepers were always intensely curious about the origins and personal affairs of their guests. Benjamin Franklin, aware of this, always stated his name, home, trade, and destination immediately when he entered a tavern. What the host learned, he remembered. Time and again a traveler recorded his astonishment at being greeted by name in a tavern where he had spent but one night previously, and that years earlier.

John Adams has left us a description of the host of the "Treadwell Tavern," at Ipswich, Massachusetts:

> As to the landlord, he is happy and as big, as proud, as conceited as any nobleman in England; always calm and good natured and lazy, but the contemplation of his farm and his sons and his house and pasture and cows, his sound judgment as he thinks, and his great holiness [he was a New Light] as well as that of his wife, [she was, also] keep him as erect in his thoughts as a noble or a prince.

Boston, New York, and Philadelphia all had many taverns, large and small. Though the small ones were mere grog shops, some of the larger ones were elegant. It is far too late for accurate comparisons, but it appears that "The Queen's Head" in New York was

The Queen's Head

one of the best. It was originally built in 1719 as the home of Etienne de Lancey. "Black Sam" Fraunces bought it in 1762 and opened it as a tavern. Sam, born on one of the islands of the West Indies, was of French ancestry, and somewhere in his early life he learned to cook with a touch that was new to the colonies. He was already well known in New York, having kept another tavern there for seven years. So his new and grander place, of brick, four square, and three and a half stories high, attracted the carriage trade at once and his cellar became famous for its superior Madeira. Concerts, banquets, and balls were held in the tavern's fine Long Room, which also saw meetings of the Sons of Liberty in 1774.

Fraunces kept "The Queen's Head" open all through the Revolutionary War and, in addition to giving needed aid to Yankee prisoners of war, probably performed other services of an even more secret nature for the rebel cause. Congress thought these valuable enough to deserve a vote of thanks and an award of two hundred pounds. In 1783 the Long Room witnessed the impressive farewell of General Washington to his officers. And in that year the name was changed to Fraunces Tavern. It still stands at Broad and Pearl Streets, restored as their headquarters by the Sons of Revolution.

Like all the best city taverns, "The Queen's Head" probably kept "fatted oxen" and other live animals on hand to be slaughtered as needed. One tavern in New York, "The Bull's Head," had no need to do this. It had the stockyards at its back door. "The Bull's Head" stood on the Bowery at what was then the edge of town and was the terminus of the Boston stage line. Not remarkably, many of its patrons were New Englanders too exhausted by six days in a stage wagon to proceed farther.

In all the large towns certain taverns served as "stations" for particular stage lines, as "The Bull's Head" did. These hostelries always kept extra horses for hire to private travelers. Men traveling alone commonly rode the hired horses and could exchange them for fresh ones at stage stops along the way. If a traveler had his wife along, he hired a post chaise and changed horses by the same system. It often took quite a while for a horse to get back to its owner.

In England a post chaise was a four-wheeled closed carriage, seating only two persons and pulled by a pair, or by four horses. A postilion drove from a saddle on one of the horses. Postilions were chosen for their light weight, as jockeys now are—hence they were usually boys. An American post chaise was simply a one-horse, two-wheeled chaise, and the man who hired it also drove it. As they could do in England, wealthy men traveling in their coaches, or chariots, could arrange to leave their own four horses at the first stage and hire fresh ones there, and at each succeeding stage, but they didn't commonly do this. A coach had seats for four, a chariot for only two. Rich men had their own postilions or, more rarely, coachmen.

As in the country, taverns in towns were gathering places for local people. This or that one had its term of extreme popularity and then faded back into obscurity at the whim of fashion. Any group wishing to raise money for a public purpose, anything from a dog pound to a college, promoted a lottery. Tickets for it were sold in taverns and the drawing of the winning numbers took place in a taproom. Dashing young "macaronis" gathered at the tavern of the moment, arriving on horseback or in "Italian" chaises. These vehicles were extraordinarily elegant because their leather tops could be folded back to display the grandeur of the driver. In the taproom or the parlour the gentlemen could entertain themselves at cards or dicing; they could play "shovel" board or billiards; and if things got too dull, a couple of them could step out back and fight a casual duel. Sometimes little plays called "drolls" were performed in taprooms. *Harlequin and Scaramouche* was popular, and so was a now-lost drama known as *Pickle Herring*. No admission was charged for the shows, but the audience was expected to express its approval with cash for the actors. Tavern servants, too, liked to be remembered. They adopted the device of an English potboy genius who put up a slotted box with the modest sign: TO INSURE PROMPTNESS. Soon after it reached the colonies, the sign read simply, T.I.P.

We can judge tavern food only from the scattered comments of people who ate it, remembering that those opinions were prejudiced both ways by the kinds of food the commentators customarily ate. Yet, astonishingly, the noted French gourmet Anthelme Brillat-Savarin was delighted with a simple Yankee meal of boiled mutton. By and large, the food seems to have been decent solid stuff in the better places, making up in quantity and variety what it may have lacked in delicacy. Roast pork, boiled beef, goose, and fish might all appear together on the same dinner table; and even breakfast was likely to include fried meat, eggs, cold gammon (pork), and a boiled hen. Vegetables appeared in all the varieties that were available; raw fruit was looked upon by many with suspicion. There was always bread, often two kinds: corn bread and wheat bread, or, in New England, "rye an' injun." Wheat didn't grow well up north, so they made do with a mixture of rye flour and cornmeal when they couldn't get wheat from the middle colonies. Coffee seems to have been uniformly bad and weak; tea, so rankly strong that it looked like coffee. All cooking was done on open fires, of course, and the meat—roasted on spits—must have been excellent when it was not tough. A Philadelphia tavern keeper advertised turnspit dogs for sale. These were a special breed developed in England: short-haired, short-legged, usually white, and trained to walk on a treadmill, or inside a large wheel, that was belted to the spit. The Pennsylvania Farm Museum owns a treadmill. Stories were told of turnspits knowing when it was time to start the roast and hiding in some unlikely spot, such as under a pew in the local church.

Though the quality of American coffee was condemned, every large center had its coffeehouses. Some of them served as taverns also, providing a few rooms for overnight

Turnspit dog

guests, and all of them sold food and liquor as well as coffee, but all of them performed basically as business exchanges. The proprietors subscribed to the newspapers, not only those of their own towns but those of distant towns, including London. They also maintained bulletin boards on which they pinned announcements of important events and of ships arriving or reported lost at sea. Most men of affairs came to their coffeehouse every day, and all came on post days, when the news from other colonies arrived. Not only did they come for needed information, they also came to trade among themselves and to parcel out shares of insurance on ships bound overseas. Each man made himself responsible up to a fixed sum and received a corresponding share of the premium paid by the ship's owner. He in turn participated in the insurance on ships owned by others of the group. In this way all shared the risks of all.

Coffeehouse

8.

Conversation in the Taproom

IT IS just past eight o'clock on a cool evening in the spring of 1751. The door closes behind five boatmen leaving the taproom and the cutting-off of their boisterous talk leaves a silence in the room, broken only by the quiet hiss and crackle of the logs in the fireplace. Candles burning on the new mantel shelf, on the bar, and on Henry Baker's old table give enough warm light to push the shadows back into the corners of the room. The big table is no longer along the front wall; it now stands out in the room with one long side facing the fire. Just now, four men with pots of ale before them are seated on stools around the end of it nearer the bar. Two are local farmers, one is a Jersey wagoner, and the fourth is a young stranger who arrived about sundown, mounted and leading a packhorse. Samuel Baker sits in his favorite armchair in front of the bar. With him around the fire are two travelers "of the better sort." All three are provided with bowls of toddy and clay pipes. Young Sam, his own pipe going nicely, leans against the bar with

his elbows resting on its shelf; Willy dozes on a stool against the wall by the desk.

Alec Boswell, who sits at the end of the long table, is into his third pot of ale and has come, as he always does, to the point of staring morosely into it. Joseph Doan, on Alec's left, and the Jersey man, opposite Joseph, are filled with curiosity about the stranger who sits next to the wagoner.

"Where's thee from, friend?" says Joseph.

"Connecticut."

"Goin' fur?"

"Jus' through the country."

"What doin'?"

"Peddlin'."

"Wacher sellin'?" Jersey asks.

"Stuff. Tinware mostly. Some notions."

"Do you work for the Pattersons, my friend?" asks the gentleman who is farthest from Samuel by the fire. The peddler turns on his stool.

"Yes, Sir, I'm an apprentice. You from up my way?"

"Boston, but I know the Pattersons." Then,

The taproom

to Samuel, "They are two Irish brothers, tin-smiths, and very enterprising men. Their shop is in a small village, but they have been able to expand it greatly by sending such men as this one far and wide to sell their goods."

"We make stuff all winter and peddle it all summer."

"Ye take country pay?" the wagoner asks.

"Yeah. Rather have that than the paper they call money. Who knows what it's worth, if anything? And what farmer'll let go of tuppence of hard money if he gets it? I trade for whatever a farmer's got: grease, lye, hides, salt meat, peach brandy, applejack. Sell it in the next village, or trade it for something lighter that'll sell; snuff or twist tobacca's good. Wot's yer trade?"

"Got a wagon 'n a team. B'long across the river in Jersey. Haul farm stuff to Philadelphia and sell it. Bring back whatever the storekeeper needs."

"And you," says the peddler, looking across the table, "you're a Quaker, ain't you?"

"I am an' I ain't—my daddy got throwed outa Meetin' fer marryin' a Baptist. I got a farm over here a coupla miles, at the end of Jericho Mountain."

"And him?" with a tilt of the head toward the end of the table.

"Farmer, too. Arsh."

"Scotch-Irish!" Alec spits out. "Joe, he laid out th' Injun Walk."

"And I hope thee is ashamed of that by now, Joseph."

"Naw, Samuel Baker, I ain't!"

"And why should he be?" Alec says. "Hadna done it he might not a'had his farm, nor I mine."

"It was an evil cheat," says Samuel.

"Nuthin' to cheatin' Injuns."

"What is this 'Indian Walk,' Mr. Baker? Nothing seems to have been heard of it in Annapolis."

"I have heard some rumor of it," says the man from Boston, "but I, too, would be glad to hear the truth of it, on its own ground."

Samuel sketches an account of the Walk and at the end of it says, "We Friends, with a few exceptions, hold that the land belongs to the Indians. If they will sell, the white man may buy at an honest price. For him to cheat them out of it, or take it from them by force, we think is criminal."

"I doubt you will ever persuade the other sects to agree with you," says Mr. Thornton, the Bostonian. "As settlers increase, both by immigration and by natural processes, they will have to have land. And they will take it as their predecessors have done. I concede it is regrettable."

"Thee is right, I reckon, but I wish thee were not."

"The whites have indeed taken it!" says Mr. Poole, the man from Annapolis. "There are still Indians in western Maryland, but only one small village remains in the eastern part of the colony. I have not seen five Indians between Annapolis and here, and I doubt that I shall see many more between here and New York."

"You go to New York on business, Mr. Poole?"

"Yes. I am a tobacco factor, buying for a London merchant. A ship carrying a consignment of mine was dismasted in a gale and limped into New York harbor. I have been unable to learn if my shipment was damaged, so it is necessary to see for myself and to arrange for reshipment if it is unhurt, which I doubt. Salt water is bad for tobacco."

"I am for Philadelphia," says Thornton. "I have some small business with Mr. Benjamin Franklin, but I go chiefly to become acquainted with the principal merchants there. I am a lawyer. Some Boston men, who retain me, are interested in the astonishing growth of Philadelphia's trade. They want me to discover if a correspondence might be of mutual benefit. Also, two of our shipbuilders want me to seek opportunities for them."

"Unless thy friends can build ships cheaper than the shipwrights here can do, thee is not likely to find work for them. There are a number of shipyards along the river and some of them are considerable enterprises."

"Can you suggest a good tavern in Philadelphia, Mr. Baker?"

"Thee might try Clark's for a night or two, but all city taverns are principally pothouses, so all of them are noisy. Thee will be better served by taking a room in a private dwelling. Ellen Burke, a worthy widow on Second Street, keeps a good house. If thee would meet the merchants, thee must go to Bradford's Coffee House, by the market. The principal men go there every day at noon."

"Thank you, Sir, I shall take your advice.

I have seen something of these rowdy pothouses with shouting and singing, with quoits, skittles, and tenpins, at all hours, and with moth-eaten wild animals on show in the yard. I notice you exhibit no curiosities here, and I approve it."

"Oh, we have our wonder," says Young Sam, chuckling. "In the morning thee must hear our ringing stone out in the wagon shed. When thee strikes it, it gives off a sound like a bell, but only if it's dry. That's why it's under the shed. There's a whole field covered with such stones a few miles up the river. No dirt there at all, just stones one on another."

"I must hear your stone. We have an excess of stones in Massachusetts, but they are all silent. This is but idle curiosity: Our speaking of taverns reminded me that I passed two just over the river on the road to your ferry. What are they? Do they trouble your trade?"

"Some but not too much," Young Sam answers. "The first thee passed is 'The Bear,' where the Penny Town road crosses. It's old, though not so old as this house. The other one, that sits just back from the bank of the river, is Garret Johnson's."

"Thank you for informing me. Will you make me another toddy, please? Perhaps these gentlemen will join me in a bowl." These gentlemen will.

"Mr. Baker," Poole says, "I was interested by those men who left here just now. Was I right in assuming that they are boatmen?"

"Yes. They are tied up here for the night and will leave at dawn. They are floating pig iron down to Philadelphia from a foundry some thirty miles above here. A rough lot, but good fellows in the main."

"I have recently heard of this new act forbidding any increase in the number of rolling mills in the colonies," said Thornton. "The ironmasters of England wish us to furnish them with iron, which they would shape and sell back to us—for hard coin, if they can get it, though we don't get coin for the raw stuff. The Crown may find the rolling mill edict hard to enforce. Will they send over half a thousand inspectors to pry into valleys and up remote creeks?"

"It will be like the old Hat Act," Poole says. "The hatters hardly glanced up from their batteries. They went on making as many hats and indenturing as many apprentices as they pleased, in direct violation. I never heard of a hatter fined for it."

"Sitting in London and trying to control people six or eight weeks away is no easy matter, especially when the controls are for the benefit of your purse at the expense of theirs," says Thornton.

Says Young Sam, as Willy serves the drinks, "A Durham man told me only yesterday of a plan to hide a new rolling mill under a gristmill and use the same water wheel. I think they're wasting their trouble, but I won't say where it is."

"A rolling mill has to have a forge, and a forge has to have a chimney," says his father. "A smoking gristmill will miss no one's attention!"

"Mr. Thornton, you mentioned Mr. Franklin," says Poole. "I have seen a pamphlet of his called *Plain Truth* with which he undertook to arouse Philadelphia to the need of being prepared to defend itself in case of attack. There are many of your sect in the town, Mr. Baker, and I am told that they are against all war. What has been the outcome?"

Young Sam answers the question. "The town raised a regiment and built two strong batteries along the river. It was time. French privateers had been seen in the bay and there was nothing to stop them from coming on up the river. Not all Quakers are against *defensive* war. I am not. James Logan was not; he gave 250 pounds to the lottery that raised the money to build the batteries."

"The consensus is against it, but it can't be denied that a good many Friends condone

Garret Johnson's ferry house (the building survives)

even offensive war," says Samuel senior. "A majority in our Assembly are Quakers, but the Assembly voted 3,000 pounds 'for flour corn and other grains' to help Governor Shirley of Massachusetts in his attack on the French in Nova Scotia. Our governor, who bought the supplies, understood, as he was meant to understand, that 'other grains' meant grains of gunpowder. And he acted accordingly."

"It's well thee was then no longer a member of the Assembly; thee would have voted against the grant."

"In plain honesty, son, I cannot be sure."

Molly Bunt mounts the steps from the kitchen carrying two candles. Erect and silent, showing little sign of the passage of time other than some increase in girth, she lights her candles from one already burning and plants them on the unoccupied end of the table. She then sets four places: two of them facing each other between the new candles, the other two in front of the peddler and the wagoner.

"Supper," she says, and starts back to the kitchen.

"I must go home to mine," says Samuel Baker, rising. "Good night, gentlemen. Pleasant journeys."

They thank him, and Mr. Poole says, "Mr. Thornton, will you share a bottle of wine with me?"

"Thank you, Sir, I shall be pleased to do so."

"Time I got along," says Joseph Doan. "Comin' Alec?"

"Comin'. No moon yet. Be black as Tophet through them woods."

Green Tree

9.

Americans Are Different

EVENTS large and small happened in the world around Bakers Ferry, but, for a few years, its people noted them without being greatly affected by them and they often failed to distinguish the large from the small. When Benjamin Franklin persuaded Philadelphians to pave Market Street, Makefield read about it and knew that the smooth round "pebbles" for the paving came from the river a few miles above the ferry. They also knew that Mr. Franklin had performed a dangerous experiment with a kite in a thunderstorm. They did not know what he was trying to do; and they didn't know how really dangerous the experiment was, nor did he. They heard, too, that he had been appointed, jointly with William Hunter, as Postmaster General for the Colonies. At the ferry it was shortly seen that the post riders, well mounted, were traveling faster than before and that they made their southbound crossings in the middle of the night. Henry B. Rundle had to haul himself out of bed to ferry them. It was just as well that Horse

had been gathered to his fathers; he couldn't have stood the pace.

England expected another war with France; and because the French held all the land to the north and west, the problem of defending the colonies loomed large. The best hope seemed to be to help the colonies to defend themselves. So, in 1754, London called for a congress at Albany, representing all the colonies. It was to discuss the means of defense and to try to form an alliance with the Six Nations of the Iroquois Indians. Franklin went as a delegate from Pennsylvania—and he went determined to persuade the congress to form a permanent colonial association. He obtained unanimous approval of the scheme from his fellow delegates, but neither the Lords of Trade in London nor any of the colonial assemblies would agree to it. While the congress was meeting, George Washington, aged twenty, was leading a Virginia expedition against the French at Fort Duquesne and was being soundly defeated by them before he got

". . . Some say an American shot him from behind,
but I think it was an Injun from behind a tree."

there. This skirmish set off the Seven Years War, known in America as the French and Indian War.

The following year General Edward Braddock arrived with a regiment of British regulars to finish off Fort Duquesne. Colonial assemblies were to furnish him with supplies and additional men. Though even the Penn family, for the first time, allowed its estates to be taxed to support the expedition, ten Quakers resigned from the Pennsylvania Assembly in protest when it voted the supplies. This turned out to be the end of the Quaker domination of the province. In Makefield Township some of the young men enlisted in militia companies to go with Braddock, and a few of the young men who did so were Quakers. The Meetings reprimanded them but didn't disown them.

General Braddock cut a useful road through the wilderness, but his refusal to listen to good advice about Indian warfare cost him all his supplies, most of his men, and his own life.

*   *   *

Richard Bascomb got down from the stage wagon at mid-morning on September 14, 1756, and entered the ferry house with the stage driver. They went at once to Young Samuel, and Richard said, "Sam, will thee pay this man my fare from Philadelphia and put it against Father's name in the book? I've got no money at all."

"Yes," said Sam, and did so. "Thee doesn't look in real good shape, Dick."

"Likely not—I walked from the Monongahela River to Philadelphia—barring a few short rides."

"Thee went out with General Braddock."

"Yeah. He's dead, and small loss. Some say an American shot him from behind, but I think it was an Injun from behind a tree."

"Thee didn't like him?"

"He was a blockhead and he was a British officer. I don't like *any* British officer!"

"What's the trouble between thee and officers?"

"Aw, our own officers ain't so bad. They

got to give orders, but they don't do it like they was givin' 'em to a dog. I don't like them red-back English sojers much, neither. They think they're better'n we are, and they don't talk English right."

"Had breakfast?" Sam asked.

"Breakfast? I ain't had supper yet!"

"Sit down."

Sam went to the kitchen door and spoke through it; then he went to a cask and drew two pots of ale. As he brought them to the

Other volunteers like Dick straggled home as best they could, but many did not return at all. The fighting moved north in a long campaign to capture Quebec. Makefield became more interested in such things as the advent of Pebbletown, a small settlement beside the Delaware, created by Philadelphia's decision to pave *all* of its main streets. The whole male population of the new hamlet worked at scraping cobblestones out of the riverbed.

table, his older son, Henry, thirteen, approached it from the kitchen door. Henry stopped and stared at the visitor's torn and dirty hunting shirt; his snagged and almost buttonless gaiters, gray with dust; and the battered remains of what had once been a hat.

"Hello, Henry, thee's growed," said Bascomb.

"Hello, Dick, *thee's* a wreck!"

"Yeah. The Frenchies beat us, or their Injuns did! Why, Molly Bunt, you get purtier all the time!"

Molly Bunt said nothing, but the skin around her eyes crinkled a little as she set cold ham, bread, and molasses before Bascomb and went back to the kitchen for tea.

* * *

* * *

In 1760, aged eighty-four, Samuel Baker finished living.

* * *

As Philadelphia grew, its need for wood increased, and quantities of it, both for lumber and for firewood, had to be supplied from ever-increasing distances. In 1764 woodsmen in the mountains began running long rafts of logs down the Delaware. They tied up overnight, but the rafts were far less maneuverable than the Durham boats and couldn't manage casual stops for rest and refreshment. Rather than allow business to drift helplessly by, tavern keepers along the river sent jugs out in skiffs to meet the rafts and quench the thirst of their crews.

Smuggling

10.

The Rumble of Thunder

WAY BACK in the 1500's a new theory had appeared—in Spain, it is said. The theory asserted that since gold would buy anything, the wealth and power of a nation depended solely upon how much of the metal it could accumulate. The practical application of the idea came to be called the Mercantile System, and the nations of Europe, large and small, applied it as practically as possible. By imposing duties on imports and at the same time paying bounties on exports, governments encouraged the making of articles that could be sold abroad and discouraged the buying of those made abroad. To further their gains, those countries that could manage to do so either conquered or settled colonies on other continents. In either case, these were not considered as actual parts of the mother country; they were simply estates, managed for her cash profit. The colony was supposed to furnish the parent nation with raw materials and to buy only what the parent manufactured. To assure this, the colony was forbidden to trade with

foreign nations. Obviously all rules were made at "home"; colonials were expected to do as they were told and say nothing. Unfortunately the Mercantile System failed to provide a way for colonies to get money with which to buy anything from anybody.

England was able to exploit her Asian and African colonies successfully in this way because she had subjugated them as a military conqueror. France did well with her colonies in North America because she settled only small areas, as bases from which to trade cheap manufactured articles to the Indians for pelts that she could sell for hard money in Europe. Aside from this trading and a little missionizing, she let the Indians alone to live their own lives. But there weren't enough Frenchmen in the trading posts to defend them, so England got all of the vast New France by taking Louisbourg and Quebec and going on to win the Seven Years War in Europe. This victory had, however, a disadvantage. The presence of France had formerly served to contain the northern and western borders of the British coastal colonies. Now the English king would have to police his own borders in order to keep land-hungry American settlers out of the new territory beyond them until he had allotted it to favored developers—and it was beyond his strength to do so.

England's trouble with her original American colonies arose from her allowing the Indians to be pushed out of them and replaced with Englishmen—to whom she applied the same rules she used elsewhere for subjugated natives. At first, the American Englishmen merely dodged. When England ordered them to trade only with her, they appeared to do so, but they also sailed south quietly and sold salt fish, flour, and slaves to the West Indies for rum and molasses, and some silver and gold money. When the Crown imposed import duties on products other than English ones, the whole east coast went into smuggling on a wholesale scale. Smugglers were not merely tolerated by their fellow colonists, they were respected. John Hancock, who led off the signing of the Declaration of Independence with a flourish, was a prominent smuggler of molasses. Earlier we overheard a hint of the Hat Act and the Iron Act—both these and some others were easily dodged. Even so, Britain was making a huge profit from her American colonies—enough, William Pitt said, to carry her through the Seven Years War.

Perhaps if King George and the entire British Parliament could have put in a year traveling through the colonies, they might have dealt more wisely with the Americans, but it is doubtful. In spite of his German ancestry, the worthy king was the perfect picture of a plump English squire, devoted to "huntin'," very sure of his rights, and incredibly stubborn. The members of Parliament were either "landed gentry," voting for nothing that might raise their taxes, or commercial men, voting for nothing that might cut their personal profits. On a dull February day in 1764, this Parliament passed the Stamp Act as a routine matter, almost unnoticed, and with it started revolution, not yet rebellion, in America. Revenue stamps had long been common in England but there the people who bought the stamps had elected the Parliament that imposed them. The same Parliament governed the American colonies; but no American sat in it and no colonist could vote for any member of it.

* * *

Young Samuel Baker, no longer actually young, raised his head from the *Gazette* and looked over his spectacles at four men who were lounging in the taproom on a rainy afternoon. The oldest of them, Henry B. Rundle, was about Sam's age, fifty-eight, but the oldest of the others had just reached twenty-two.

"Says here the people won't buy those stamps at all. Up in Boston some men that call themselves 'The Sons of Liberty' roughed up the British Crown agent and made him swear an oath never to sell a stamp!"

"What kind of stamps?" asked Sam's son Henry.

"Tax stamps. They're supposed to be stuck on newspapers, broadsides, and any kind of legal paper."

"What's agin 'em?" asked Moses Doan. "Mose" was Joseph Doan's son; at the age of nineteen he stood six feet two inches tall, was black-haired, and had a handsome bony face with a hawk nose and dark eyes that gleamed under thick eyebrows. His shoulders were wide and his chest deep. It was said that Mose Doan could jump clear over a sixteen-hand horse. He had four brothers and three cousins nearly as active and fine looking as he was.

"Taxes, that's what's against 'em," said Sam. "These Sons of Liberty say that Parliament can tax the people that elected it, but nobody over here elected any member; so it hasn't any right to tax Americans."

"Damfi see that!" said Mose. "Parliament is th' gummunt, ain't it?"

"Wel-l," said Henry B., "we're English right enough, but our own Assembly taxes us, and we elect it; we cert'ny don't elect Parliament. Let it tax England and leave us be!"

"Benjamin Franklin said something"— Sam searched the column before him. "Hum, here it is: 'British subjects, by removing to America, do not thereby lose their native rights!'"

"Hufalutin," Mose said, "I don't need no stamps, but if I did, I'd buy 'em!"

"I wouldn't!" said Henry B.

"Neither'd I," said Giles Boswell.

"Nor me neither," said Henry Baker.

"Well," said Young Sam, "I guess I wouldn't either."

* * *

The Stamp Act brought the thirteen colonies together as nothing else had been able to do before. When American notables spoke out against it, newspapers everywhere reported their speeches in full. Farmers read them or heard them discussed in places like the ferry house. In towns the coffeehouses seethed with the argument, and artisans everywhere formed chapters of the Sons of Liberty. Why, said an astounded London, should the Americans object to a tax that amounts to only a shilling a year per man? The Americans weren't objecting to the shilling; it was "taxation without representation" that stuck in their collective craw.

A congress that represented most of the colonies met in New York. It was notable only because it was the first of its kind; its proceedings were mostly talk. But the colonials had learned the strength of union and they got together to apply muscle. American merchants owed debts in England amounting to four million pounds. They refused to pay a penny of them until the Stamp Act was repealed. Further, those who had placed orders for goods in London canceled the orders. Many English factories had to shut down; ships lay idle in English harbors; workmen hopelessly sought jobs. Parliament had to repeal the Stamp Act, but its damage had been done. America quieted down, but for the next ten years every act of Parliament that dealt with the colonies was resented. "No taxation without representation" became "no legislation without representation." Still, until the ten years had nearly ended, nobody mentioned independence. Conservatives and radicals alike remained loyal to King George. But "the commoner sort" had begun to feel its oats and the old respect for the gentry was breaking down; the gentry said it was "barbarous."

The great East India Company found itself with warehouses full of unsold tea; so the Crown remitted the taxes owed by the company on the tea and granted the company a monopoly on selling it in America. Even with its three-pence-a-pound import tax, paid by the buyer, this tea was cheaper than smuggled tea. Hence it undersold all the regular merchants, who eagerly joined with the radicals in denouncing it.

* * *

Young Sam Baker was not as long-lived as his father had been. In 1774 the executors of his will sold his ferry and tavern to

Samuel McConkey, a Scotch-Irish Presbyterian who lived in Bucks County, possibly at Newtown. McConkey had previously bought Johnson's ferry, on the New Jersey side of the river, and the farm that went with it, including the ferry house, but he rented that to James Slack, who had run it for some years previously. It seems that Sam McConkey preferred to invest in property and let someone else do the work on it. He found a man named Cadwalader to run the Baker ferry for him; and he persuaded Henry Baker to remain in charge of the Baker tavern, with Henry's younger brother, Samuel, Jr., to help him. This lad was actually Samuel the third, but he was always known as Samuel, Jr.

* * *

"Henry Baker," said Richard Yardley after Meeting, "is thee serving tea at thy tavern these days?"

"Not a drop! I wouldn't if I could get it, and I think none can be bought. The ships weren't allowed to unload it at Philadelphia."

"Nor at New York, either," said Yardley. "And I have just learned that the Boston Sons of Liberty and, it is hinted, some men of affairs with them, boarded three tea ships and threw their cargoes into the harbor! British men of war have now closed the port there. The people are in need of food and have appealed to all the colonies for help."

"The wheat crop looks good. We could send them some presently."

"There is a movement afoot to do so. I shall contribute to it and it seems that thee will, also, but there are many in this county who will not."

"Yes. They're afraid of trouble and quite a few think that Parliament has a right to dictate to us. Where's the grain going to be collected?"

"At Newtown. There's a committee there. But not, of course, until the wheat has cured enough to be sent. It will go in wagons. Ships may not go into Boston but the roads are open."

* * *

The colonies now realized that what injured one of them injured all; so they appointed delegates, representing the whole "continent," to assemble and decide what could be done to protect the rights of the people *as British subjects.*

* * *

Makefield Meeting House

The first Continental Congress met at Philadelphia in September 1774. It forbade all trade with England and created a loose organization known as the "Association" to enforce the decree. Committees of the Association were formed in every town to expose all "foes of the rights of British America." The radical enforcers were "Patriots"; their conservative quarry became "Tories." The committees exercised their own judgment. Tories, or men the patriot committees decided were Tories, had their property destroyed and were often treated to a coat of tar and feathers and given a ride on a fence rail. Not infrequently, a man was denounced as a Tory simply because a Committee member had a personal grudge against him. It amounted, as Samuel Seabury said, to an inquisition—but Seabury was vilified for saying it.

* * *

In April 1775, as the first delegates to the second Continental Congress were beginning to arrive in Philadelphia, the British general Thomas Gage sent 800 men out from Boston to seize military stores that his spies had discovered in Concord. The pa-triots had spies, too; they had moved the stores. Gage's men never got to Concord. Two of the American spies, William Dawes and Paul Revere, warned the countryside that the British were coming, and when Gage's men reached Lexington, they were met by a blast of musket fire that forced them back to Boston.

Special messengers carried the news of the skirmish through the whole country. Many, though by no means all, who had clung to loyalty became patriots overnight. Many patriots, who were by no means radicals, began to talk openly of independence. King George himself had lighted that torch by announcing that he would use foreign help to suppress the American rebellion, because it was obviously aimed at independence. The report of this speech reached the colonies at just about the time that Tom Paine published *Common Sense,* in January 1776. Paine demanded independence in simple, forceful language, and everybody in the colonies read it or heard it: "To know whether it be the interest of this continent to be Independent, we need only to ask this simple question: Is it the interest of a man to be a boy all his life?"

*   *   *

"If the King wants to put down a rebellion, he picked the best way to start one. Attack a man and he'll fight back," said Henry Baker, sitting in his grandfather's old chair by the fire.

"I'm ready," said Sam, Jr., from behind the bar. "It's time we Americans ran our own affairs."

"Remember, thee's a Friend," said his brother. "Friends don't fight."

"Some have, though; and some will again."

"I'd regret it, but I couldn't try to stop thee. I have thought of it myself, I admit. The time has come to cut our leading strings and I fear only war can do it."

"I'm a Quaker, too, as near as nuthin'," said Mose Doan, "but if it comes to a fight, I'll fight—for the King! And there's plenty more in Bucks County that'll do the same, and don't you forgit it. Yeah! I think we oughta have a chance to send men to Parliament, but we don't have to rebel against the King to get it. That's treason and the King'll show you 'tis! A bunch of farmers can't fight British reg'lars! They'll run at the first volley." Mose delivered his last words with the tavern door open and he slammed it for emphasis as he left.

"They didn't run at Lexington," Henry said. "But he's right that there are more Tories than Whigs here."

Sam McConkey spoke: "Much noise and little wool, as the Devil said when he sheared his pig!"

But Sam was wrong.

11.

Rebellion

THE NEW ENGLAND patriot militia, with no single leader, had surrounded Boston and put it under siege. The British took one famous hill from them at such cost in lives that a patriot captain wished he might sell them some more hills at the same price. Militia companies from the other colonies moved to Boston as fast as they could walk, and George Washington, newly commissioned by Congress as Commander in Chief of all American forces, soon arrived with three other fledgling generals and took charge. In late February 1776 Washington was able to mount field guns on Dorchester Heights, where he could shell the city from a position too high for the English guns to reach, even when the rear wheels of their gun carriages were lowered into trenches. General William Howe, who had replaced Gage, put his redcoats aboard the ships in the harbor and took them to Halifax. The Yankee army marched to New York. Though the town was smaller than Boston or Philadelphia, Congress thought it important to prevent its capture, both to keep up the

people's spirits and to keep the British from controlling the Hudson and so cutting New England off from the rest of the colonies.

On June 7, 1776, Richard Henry Lee of Virginia moved in the second Continental Congress that "these United Colonies are, and of right ought to be free and independent states." The delegates debated for the rest of the month before the motion was carried. Thomas Jefferson wrote out their decision for them in stately language. Without regard for the safety of their necks ("We must hang together, or assuredly we shall hang separately") they signed it; and on the fourth of July they published it.

* * *

Fifty British warships brought General Howe and his army, reinforced with hired Hessian troops, into New York Bay on June 29. On the day that the Declaration of Independence was published, they encamped on Staten Island, where the general set up his headquarters. On that same fourth of July, our Tory acquaintance Moses Doan

Mose Doan and General Howe

and his brother, Levi, left home and struck across New Jersey. Levi went to York Island, as they called Manhattan, to sell six allegedly stolen horses and no doubt to see what he could see. Mose went straight to British headquarters, where he must have been expected, because he was taken at once to General Howe.

The general sent him across the bay to Long Island to discover the lay of the land and find out what the rebel army was doing there. Such maps as existed were undependable. In his country clothes, Mose could go anywhere without arousing suspicion. Howe knew that the easy way to get into New York was from Brooklyn, across the narrow East River. The Yankees knew it, too, and Mose discovered that they had blocked the river with sunken boats to keep warships out of it—and they had also fortified a strong position on Brooklyn Heights.

On August 22, 1776, General Howe moved most of his army across the bay to Long Island and set up camp within rifle shot of a

line of hills that lay a mile and a half south of the American forts. General Israel Putnam, commanding the American forces, sent strong detachments forward to man the hills. General William Alexander Stirling's rebel troops formed the right wing of these, guarding the shore where Howe's main attack was expected. American General John Sullivan covered the center, where a road from Flatbush cut through a pass to intersect the east-west road from Brooklyn to Jamaica. A smaller force of Yankees under an officer with the curious name of Wills Wylls held the left. The Jamaica road ran through the valley between the two ridges and hence between the advance troops and their base on Brooklyn Heights.

The two sides glared at each other for five days during which nothing happened except that Yankee riflemen "assassinated" (as the British said) a few officers in the English camp. Then, during the night of August 26–27, Mose Doan guided Generals James Clinton and Charles Cornwallis, and ten thousand British regulars, with fourteen field guns, in a wide swing to the east and brought them in from the American left on the Jamaica Road. Mose knew this approach was almost unguarded. The redcoats quietly captured the five mounted men who had been sent out to reconnoiter in that direction.

Up on Brooklyn Heights, at nine o'clock on the morning of the twenty-seventh, George Washington heard a cannon go off on the right, where Stirling was stationed, and assumed that the attack he expected there had begun. At the signal, for it was that, a small force attacked Stirling, and the Hessians in front of Sullivan in the center charged up the slope at his troops. Almost at that moment a messenger rushed up to tell Sullivan that the main British force was behind him! All the Americans began a headlong rush back to Brooklyn Heights. Stirling's men had to flounder through a marsh. Sullivan's were badly mauled and none would have escaped at all if one brigade of Maryland regulars had not bought a path for them at a deadly price. Sullivan and

Stirling were both captured, but they were soon exchanged for British officers held by the Americans, as was customary at the time.

The survivors in the fort expected an immediate attack, but to their astonishment the British marched smartly back to their camp. Howe, an excellent general, knew he didn't have men enough to storm so strong a position. Under cover of darkness, rain, and fog, Washington removed his men from the Heights and had them ferried across the East River to Manhattan, which, by now, he knew he could not hold. This was the beginning of a long discouraging retreat: out of New York to Harlem Heights, where he mistakenly left little Fort Washington, manned, behind him and moved on north to White Plains and then to Peekskill. Here he crossed the Hudson on November 12 and turned southward. Sickness ravaged the Yankee forces; and the medical department was one good doctor over a rabble of quacks who would take no orders from him. Militiamen, weary of war, simply went home by the thousands, and desertions from the

Retreat from Brooklyn Heights

Continental regulars became common. Even worse, the regulars had enlisted for short terms and many of the terms were running out. Sometimes the commanding general's headquarters had no record of when they ran out. Gloom and pessimism ran through the new states; had news not traveled so slowly, they would have had even worse misgivings.

The British easily overran Fort Washington and took 3,000 prisoners. Then they crossed the Hudson at night and started after General Washington. He evacuated Fort Lee, so fast that hot cooking pots had to be left behind, and rushed his troops across the one open bridge over the Hackensack River. The enemy would have reached the bridge before him if they hadn't been confused in their geography.

Only a day or so ahead of the redcoats, Washington passed through Newark and Elizabethtown. He reached New Brunswick on November 29 with a ten-mile lead, but the British soldiers were tired and he got out safely and pressed on toward Princeton and Trenton. By now he was planning ahead—he needed to get another river between his troops and the enemy.

At some time, near New Brunswick, the general got in touch with an old acquaintance, John Honeyman, who lived nearby at Griggstown. Honeyman agreed to pretend to "turn Tory"—no unusual thing for a man to do just then in New Jersey—and with that

The Mercereau brothers

as a cover, to spy on the British. Washington made it good. He denounced Honeyman as a British spy and offered a reward for his capture *alive*, but he gave Honeyman's wife a warrant of security that protected her and her children "from all harm and annoyance from any quarter." She had to make use of it, too, when local patriot hotheads harassed her. The document must have astonished them.

John was by trade a weaver and butcher. He had good Tory credentials. He had been a British soldier—a member of General James Wolfe's bodyguard at Quebec. That experience made him a knowledgeable spy but did not keep him from becoming a staunch patriot. As a blind for spying, he practiced his butchering; he bought cattle and sold meat to the English and German troops. Sometimes he picked up horses to sell to officers. Officers have information.

General Washington had decided to take his army into Pennsylvania to rest and to await reinforcements from the north—and he did not want the British to be able to follow him. To effect this, he sent a Colonel Humpton, a Pennsylvanian, ahead to commandeer all the boats on the Delaware, with special attention to Durham boats, and to move them across to the Pennsylvania shore. The colonel found help in two brothers, Joshua and John Mercereau; boatmen and boat builders on the Jersey side of the river, they knew every island and creek along it. They not only found every visible craft for twenty miles along the stream, they also found those that the Tories had hidden and sunk for the use of General Cornwallis, who had also sent an advance agent to the area.

General William Maxwell took charge of the Mercereau boats and hid them behind islands and in creeks on the Pennsylvania side. Many were packed in behind Malta Island (now Smith's) about a mile below Coryells Ferry. Maxwell sent some boats quite far up the river to be used for bringing over the troops of General Charles Lee.

General Sterling's headquarters

Washington had ordered this considerable force, still in northern New Jersey, to join him on the Delaware, but Lee disregarded the order with the idea of first bringing off a brilliant victory that would prove him to be the man who should command the whole army.

Washington, the man who did command it, reached Trenton on December 3. He sent all his army's baggage across the river immediately but kept the troops on the Jersey side for five days longer. When he learned that Howe and Cornwallis were advancing with an enlarged force, he sent the men over, apparently on the regular ferries that operated there. As the last patriot troops embarked, Howe entered the town behind them. Both he and Cornwallis, who arrived on the bank opposite Coryells Ferry, were completely frustrated by the lack of any means to cross the river.

General Washington set up temporary headquarters in a mansion not far from the ferry landing in Pennsylvania. He disposed his troops along the river to guard against a British crossing and to get some much-needed rest. Large and small groups of log huts, and some tents, stretched from below

Bristol to Coryells Ferry. After a few days the general moved his headquarters north and inland to the farmhouse of William Keith on the road from Newtown to Thompson's mill, which had originally been Pidcock's.

Pidcock's old house, enlarged by Thompson, became headquarters for General Stirling, who, along with Sullivan, had been exchanged by the British. The group at the house with Stirling was a more distinguished one than its members could have known. Aside from the fact that the general himself, born plain William Alexander, claimed a Scottish earldom and was commonly called Lord Stirling, Tom Paine, equipped with a musket, was in the house as a sort of guest of the army, a very valuable guest. Captain William Washington, a brave and able kinsman of the Commander in Chief, was there; so was Lieutenant James Monroe, all of eighteen years old, who, in forty years, would be President of the United States.

* * *

On December 13 Congress decided that the British were too close to Philadelphia for comfort, so it departed as a body to Baltimore. A few days later General Howe returned to the delights of New York for the winter, taking Cornwallis' English troops with him and leaving Princeton, Trenton, and Burlington garrisoned with a brigade each of Hessians who assumed that fighting was over for the winter, as it would have been under the customs of warfare in Europe.

* * *

Perhaps it was on December 17: Tom Paine sat down before the fireplace of the Pidcock-Thompson kitchen and wrote by the light of a tallow dip. He wrote strong pungent words which, in that day of flowery language, it seems only he could write. When his essay was finished, he took it to Philadelphia and it appeared in the *Pennsylvania Evening Post* for December 19. Early that morning a special courier filled his saddlebags with copies of the paper and brought them to Washington's headquarters. The general read the article at noon and had copies distributed through the camps with orders that *The Crisis* be read to every corporal's guard: *"These are the times that try men's souls. The summer soldier and the sunshine patriot will in this crisis, shrink from the service of his country, but he that stands it NOW deserves the thanks of men and women. Tyranny, like Hell, is not easily conquered . . ."*

* * *

Officers in the Continental Army were generally from well-to-do families and they dressed accordingly. Their uniforms were well tailored and were often replaced as they wore out. Some few elite troops, like Washington's bodyguards, wore smart uniforms, but most of the foot soldiers wore any clothes they could scrape together, and they could rarely replace anything. Their commonest outer garment was a "rifle" shirt of unbleached linen, patterned on the frontiersman's hunting shirt and hence usually made

with fringed seams and capped shoulders; often having a turn-over collar but sometimes lacking it. The shirt, shaped somewhat like a thigh-length coat without buttons, was worn outside the breeches. In a sense it was double-breasted, lapping over in front and belted with leather at the waist. Men wore these shirts in summer with little or nothing under them; in winter they put them on over whatever warm clothes they had. They were tough garments; nevertheless by this time most of the rifle shirts along the Delaware were in ruins and the shreds of many now served to swab musket barrels. All but a comparative handful of these men had been fighting and running since July and quite a few had been under arms since the previous winter.

Now winter was upon them and all thought of appearances was abolished by the basic need to keep warm. Men made makeshift coats out of old blankets—some of them crudely tailored, others worn poncho-fashion, with a hole in the middle for the head. The piece that came out of the hole was likely to be tortured into serving as a cap.

To give a cocked hat's brim its jaunty upsweep, it had first to be steamed, then tied into shape with strings, then dried in a slow oven. The procedure was difficult under military conditions. Even officers, perhaps even the Commander in Chief himself, had trouble keeping their hats in shape—and most of theirs were expensive beavers. The hats of the rankers, if they survived, were made of wool felt, or at best rabbit fur, held together with shellac. Though these, too, had started with the three-cornered shapes of cocked hats, the rains of New York and New Jersey had long since relaxed their brims to drooping disks with undulant edges.

But a hat, though desirable for a soldier, is far less important to him than a stout pair of shoes. No doubt most of the volunteers had such footwear when they enlisted— good handmade cowhide clodhoppers with

double-thick soles—but months of putting one ahead of the other had wrecked them. There were cobblers in every village and some were attached to the army, but the soldiers had had little time to pause for repairs, and in most cases no money to pay for them. Plenty of the men were handy enough to do crude patching for themselves, but they could do little without leather and there was a limit to what of that could be filched from issued equipment. So there were feet that had no better protection than wrappings of burlap that constantly worked loose and that would wear through in a ten-mile march.

*   *   *

History says little of the accomplishments of the Continental Army's commissary, but they were continuously heroic. Here in Bucks County, Washington placed the commissary headquarters at Newtown, more or less equidistant from all the camps along the river. At the start there were perhaps 4,000

men to feed. Recruiting and reinforcement gradually doubled the number. Almost the only source of supply was the immediate countryside. It was up to the commissary to find meat, flour, and cornmeal, and to pay for it with the nearly worthless paper money that Congress printed. Many Tory millers in Bucks County refused to sell flour and meal to the army at any price; so the commander was forced, against his principles, to give the commissary power to take supplies by force.

There is something in adversity that stiffens resolution. Astonishingly, the morale of the soldiers was high, but their spirit emphatically did not extend to the general public. The Patriots' confidence in ultimate victory was near the lowest ebb and was not strengthened by the flight of Congress from Philadelphia. George Washington realized that only a spectacular stroke could save the American cause. It would have to be successful, of course, and it would have to be brought off quickly, because the enlistments of most of the seasoned troops would expire

83

at the year's end. These included not only the bulk of the men he had brought to the Delaware, and the majority of those he had ordered in from the Canadian border and from the upper Hudson valley, but most of General Lee's troops in New Jersey. Lee had failed to bring off his grandstand play, and was about ready to obey orders and start south, when he left his camp to spend an evening with a lady friend. The British captured him in her house. General Sullivan posted north and brought Lee's troops into Pennsylvania.

Washington never told anyone just when he made up his mind to attack Trenton; it was heard of as a rumor in Philadelphia on December 18, but no hint of it had reached the British. By that time Washington and General Nathanael Greene were planning tactics in Greene's quarters at the Merrick farm. This was next to the commander's own headquarters at Keith's, and Washington had had part of the fence removed between the two places so that he could easily get to Merrick's and meet with Greene in privacy. William Keith was elderly and was possessed by simple curiosity that made him a nuisance. But the general must have had some way of protecting himself from Keith at need; it is known that he talked with at least two people in his own headquarters without allowing a whisper of what was said to be known—then or since.

* * *

On December 22 (notice that he knew just when to do this) John Honeyman spotted two American scouts hiding in a hedge north of Trenton. John made a great ado of chasing a cow in the adjacent field. He shouted at

The "capture" of Honeyman

her and cracked a whip and finally drove her near the hedge. There he conveniently slipped on a patch of ice and fell. The scouts jumped on him at once. John put up a convincing fight but surrendered when one of the men put a pistol to his head. The scouts almost certainly knew who he was because they obeyed orders and took him directly to headquarters. Washington ordered everybody out of the room, and he and Honeyman talked alone for half an hour. One can only guess that John reported the number of Hessians quartered in Trenton, the number of field guns there, and the positions of the guard posts around the town. The general had seen the place, but doubtless he queried

The talk ended around sunset. The "prisoner" was locked in a small outbuilding behind the Keith house to be held for court-martial in the morning. Guards stood at the door. Someone *had* to have been let in on the secret. Soon after dark, one of the huts that sheltered the commander's bodyguard caught fire. A great hullabaloo arose and Honeyman's guards *left their posts* to help fight the flames. They could have been shot for this, but they were not even court-martialed. When they returned to the prison, the door was open and of course John Honeyman had left. One story claims that General Washington himself opened the door. It seems unlikely.

Honeyman's "escape"

his spy about details of its streets and hills, the disposition of military stores, and the location of the headquarters of Colonel Johann Gotlieb Rall, the commander of the Hessian garrison. If Washington paid Honeyman with the gold and silver coins that spies usually got for their services, he must have used the last such money his headquarters had, or else used his personal funds, because within a week he asked the Philadelphia financier Robert Morris for hard money "to pay certain people."

Free of his lockup, John was by no means in the clear. He was still branded as a Tory spy and in any reasonable direction his way of escape lay through the Yankee camp. The shortest distance from Keith's to the bank of the Delaware was more than two miles. The river was guarded and he had to get across it. We are at liberty to guess that he had help, because he did get across and made his way back to Trenton. There he gave the Hessian commander, Colonel Rall, a not quite full account of his "capture" and "escape" and told the colonel that the Americans were in bad condition, far too bad to attempt an attack on him. "Merry Christmas, Colonel!" John left for New Brunswick; it seemed a good idea to be out of the way.

* * *

It is Christmas Eve. Darkness has fallen. At the Merrick house, General Washington and his major generals are completing plans for the attack. With them is Captain Cornelius Coryell, John's son, upon whom they depend for information about geography—he is their detailed map and will be their guide. Captain Coryell's sixteen-year-old son, George, also appeared at Merrick's that evening and was given instructions by the commander.

* * *

At the small house of John Tomlinson on Jericho Mountain, less than two miles from the meeting of the generals, Tomlinson and Moses Doan are eating supper. Mose will sleep here tonight. He has spent the day, as he has spent several days, lurking on the fringes of the Yankee camps. He has moved carefully because he is on home ground where plenty of people would know him at sight. He is now sure that something is up, but he doesn't know just what it is. He has correctly reported the number and distribution of the American forces to the British General James Grant at New Brunswick; and today Grant has written to Colonel von Donop, at Princeton, warning him that Trenton may be attacked.

Mose has become the active leader of a Tory band usually called simply "The Doans." In addition to Mose, the band includes four of his brothers—Aaron, Levi, Mahlon, and Joseph—and their cousin Abraham, who is said to resemble Mose as closely as an identical twin. The band also includes a few more distant family connections and

some other young men of ardent Tory sympathies. John Tomlinson is an undercover member. He is thought by some to be the organizing brain behind the Doans' activities. All members act as spies, saboteurs, and mounted guerrillas, serving the British cause in any way they can. One way is by attacking supply wagons on their way to the American camps. Another is by distributing the almost undetectable counterfeit Continental money that has been shipped over from London to further dilute the value of the real stuff. Bucks County Tories use quantities of it to pay the triple taxes that are levied on them. The Doans know who the local tax collectors are, and when they think one of them has accumulated a considerable sum, they abstract it from him at gunpoint. In their activities, if an occasional needed horse be excepted, the Doans steal nothing but what belongs to "the Congress." Tories in Bucks County help them and hide them at need.

* * *

In the "Woods Camp," so-called because it is literally in the forest, just north of Bowmans Hill, three young men are squatting around the fireplace of a crude log hut they have built for themselves. They are members of Captain van Horn's company of Bucks County militia and their regular duty is manning the observation post that General Stirling has set up in a tall pine tree on the hilltop. The inside of their hut is about twelve feet by nine with a small door near the front corner at the fireplace end. The other end, and most of both side walls, are filled by their bunks, low platforms made of poles. There is no other furniture. Each man's gun rests above his bunk across two pegs driven into the wall, and from the same pegs hang his other military equipment: powder horn, bullet pouch, bayonet, axe, hunting knife, knapsack, and canteen. Two of the guns are muskets; the third is a long rifle.

The fireplace is a low alcove made of field-stones piled without mortar. A long flat stone serves as a lintel across its top. Smoke escapes through the opening behind the lintel; there is no chimney. Other flat stones make a hearth and just now, greased with a little pork fat, they are serving as a griddle to cook a row of corn dodgers. A cast-iron pot, hung from a fresh-cut green pole that lies across the top of the fireplace behind the lintel, is boiling briskly. This pot, three wooden bowls, and three pewter spoons complete the "kitchen" equipment, unless one includes three sharpened sticks with their bark left on. These are in use at the moment for broiling chunks of extremely fresh beef over the fire.

Captain van Horn's company has only recently been mustered into the army; hence the clothes of the three around the fire are in much better shape than those of the veterans. In fact, two of them are wearing garments that against this background are conspicuously new. They are conscious of this and have deliberately dampened their hats to relax their three-cornered shape. These two are Benjamin Taylor, from down Dolington way, and Sam Baker, Jr., from

the ferry house. Quakers, both, they are trying with little success to avoid using the plain language. The third man, a couple of years older than they, is Duncan MacNab, the owner of the rifle. Duncan is a Scot from North Carolina. His clothes, though noticeably worn, are yet in far better shape than is usual in this army. He has had no need to dampen his hat—it is a coonskin cap.

"Hold ma meat, Ben." Duncan picks up two of the pewter spoons and deftly uses their flat handles to flip the thick corn cakes over. "How many of these things do ya reckon we need fer three days?"

"Better cook up all the meal we've got, except enough to make mush for breakfast. Then thee won't have to count," Sam Baker says. "Somebody'll steal what we leave in the cabin anyway. Think this meat's done?"

"Yeah, try it."

"Hot!"

"Tough!" says Ben. "Couldn't stick a fork in the gravy."

"No gravy."

"No fork."

"Little gravy'd be good on these yere dodgers."

"That ol' cow's too much for me," Sam,

Jr., says. "I can't finish her. She couldn't a been one of Henry's cows. He don't let 'em get that old."

"Throw her in the pot with the rest; she'll be tender by mornin'."

"My father's got no cows left; army's taken 'em all," Taylor says.

"Paid fer 'em, warn't he?"

"Yeah. With Congress paper."

The three light clay pipes, short ones with reed stems. The two Quakers ease themselves onto the ends of the nearest bunks while Duncan continues to cook corn dodgers, dipping water from a wooden pail by the door and mixing meal with it in small batches in a bowl.

"What does thee—what do you suppose is up?" says Baker. "Parade tomorrow. And every man to carry *three days'* rations?"

"We're shore goin' somewheres. At least our ole cow won't go bad in this weather."

"Maybe we're going to try something on the Dutchmen at Princeton, or Trenton."

"Trenton'd be easiest. We could come in on 'em downhill. Closer, too."

"Dunk, what's a tarheel like thee doing in a Pennsylvania company?"

"Ahm no ta'heel! Ah live in the hills west in No'th Ca'lina; the ta'heels is in the swamps, east. Ah come up heah to look around. Ah run outta eatin' money an went to work for Richahd Yahdley. No sense goin' back down home to jine up when Ah could do it right heah."

"Did thee just come north out of curiosity?"

"Well, no. Mah granpappy took up land heah'bouts and then left it an' struck west. Ah figgered to find it, an' see if it's still ourn. When this fracas is over, Ah'll go on lookin'."

"Maybe we can help thee find it, then. We'd better get some sleep."

"Thankee Sam, Ah'd be glad of it."

"Yeah, sleep. I'm glad the redbacks won't be able to see that parade tomorrow."

George Coryell in Trenton

WHITE STAR

12.

Christmas Day

AT DAWN on December 25, young George Coryell took a horse across the Delaware on his grandfather's ferry and followed the roads south to Trenton. He had no need to conceal himself; plenty of other civilians were taking the same roads to the same place that day. General Howe had recently announced that all rebels who signed a form pledging their allegiance to the king would be forgiven their transgressions. Many frightened Whigs were heading for Trenton to sign up, and just to be on the safe side, a lot of Tories were signing the forms, too.

George noted that there were no Hessian guards along the river anywhere above Trenton. Though the normal outposts around the town were manned, the sentries questioned no one entering or leaving. This may have been partly due to language difficulties. The place was full of form signers and off-duty Hessian soldiers who were interested only in a rousing German celebration of Christmas. George was able to ride, unnoticed, anywhere he wished. He saw two woodenly immobile sentries standing at parade rest outside Colonel Rall's headquarters, but he saw no other military activity.

The young spy was obliged to ride all the way back to Coryells Ferry, where he was known and expected, even though it would have saved him six miles to cross at McConkeys, or at Beaumonts, which landed at the end of the road to Keith's farm. Both boy and horse were tired when they reached headquarters in the early afternoon. George reported to General Washington personally and in private. Whether he merely gave an overall account of what he had seen or told the general something more specific isn't known. He went home and, almost immediately after he left to go there, a mounted messenger took off from headquarters in haste for an unknown destination. George Washington remained silent about many matters of this sort for the rest of his life.

* * *

Only parts of the 8,000 American troops along the Delaware were to engage in the

Trenton project—a total of about 2,400, more than half of them from the Woods Camp, would make the main attack. Brigadier General John Cadwalader was ordered to cross the Delaware, with another 1,800 men, some miles below Trenton and to cut the road to Burlington, where more Hessians were quartered. Brigadier General James Ewing was to bring still another 600 or so across immediately below Trenton to block the town's escape route to the south, which was the bridge over Assunpink Creek.

Colonel John Glover and his fisherman-soldiers from Marblehead, Massachusetts, began the job of moving the hidden boats down to McConkeys Ferry on the sunny morning of the twenty-fifth. Soon after noon the men at the Woods Camp began a march to the same point. Clouds gathered as they started, the air became raw, and the temperature hovered just above freezing.

* * *

Moses Doan left Tomlinson's late on Christmas morning because he knew he had time to kill. From a concealed lookout on the eastern end of Jericho Mountain, he saw artillery and some infantry moving down the River Road. On the river, Durham boats were slipping downstream at the water's speed. Mose left his lookout and rode upriver, keeping well back from the hutments but staying near enough to them to see the stir of activity at Camp Woods. Something was up all right—and Mose thought he knew what it was, but he had to be sure.

He rode on up the river a few miles to Howells Ferry. There he hid his horse in an abandoned cabin and fed him. In response to Doan's signal, a watching Tory rowed a bateau over, brought Mose across, and provided him with another horse. Mose moved slowly downstream, keeping near the bank but out of sight from the opposite shore. He was sure the rebels would make no real move until dark, so he stopped to rest at a little alehouse where he knew an old woman

who ran the place. She fed him but she had no information to give.

* * *

Daylight was failing by the time the ranks came to attention on the field in front of the McConkey ferry house. The air became colder and a nasty mixture of snow and sleet began to fall. It seems doubtful that the "parade" was anything more than an assembly to account for all units. It was held in near-silence. By order, every officer had attached a piece of white paper to the front of his hat for identification in the dark. General Washington and his immediate subordinates—Generals Greene, Sullivan, Knox, Stirling, Mercer, and Stephen—arrived in time to review the muster. When it was over, they all went into the tavern for an early supper.

Darkness came on and the air became colder. Sleet had started freezing on tree branches and a keen easterly wind drove the stuff into the faces of the men waiting stolidly for their turn to embark. Several boats had already put out when Captain van Horn brought his company to attention, right-faced it, and marched it down to the shore in a column of twos. A platoon of Glover's men, some of them with pierced tin lanterns, directed the loading. The Durham boats were grounded against the bank side by side. Ice had formed around them and was thickening rapidly.

Upstream from the foot soldiers' boats, General Knox's artillerymen sweated and swore in the cold as they labored to roll the wheels of the last of their eighteen field pieces up gangplanks and onto temporary decks laid across a pair of Durham boats that were lashed together. Some of the guns had been loaded earlier on the ferryboats that normally served McConkeys and Beaumonts Ferries. Other gangplanks led to boats set aside for artillery draft horses and officers' mounts. According to legend, one of the artillery catamarans upset and dumped its burden into the river.

"Left file, port side; right file, starboard," said the Marblehead guide. "Wade out and climb over the side."

"Wait half an hour and we could all walk across," said Ben Taylor as he broke through the shore ice. "We might even swim; we certainly couldn't get any wetter."

"Wonder if th' Old Hoss'll have to wade, too?" Duncan said, carefully placing his rifle in the boat and climbing in after it. "Old Hoss" was the rankers' name for their Commander in Chief.

"Shove off!" came quietly from the corporal in charge of the boat. "You men sit still, and keep your hands off the footways or we'll step on 'em."

Three of the guides pushed the boat into the stream. A squad of Glover's fishermen began the old routine of setting the poles and walking the boat past them. They used

92

the poles on the downstream side only, lifting them at the stern and crossing over to carry them forward on the upstream side. The footways had wooden cleats nailed across them to give the polemen better traction, but, glazed with sleet as they were, the cleats didn't help much. Out in the stream the boat met floating chunks of ice that did nothing to make poling easy. This ice, up to six inches thick, had been freed by a thaw far up the river. In spite of the corporal's order, the troopers tried to help by leaning over the sides to push the ice away with their musket butts. They succeeded only in interfering with the polers, who couldn't easily see what was going on. The corporal, steering with a long oar, aft, could hold the course only by guess; he could see nothing a boat's length ahead, and could avoid colliding with other boats only by listening to the sounds that came from them. But the other shore was not far away, and wherever they hit it, they landed.

"So this is Jersey! Fust tahm Ah wuz evah heah," Duncan said as they struggled up the slippery bank after a voyage of nearly an hour.

"Fall in!" said the sergeant, keeping his voice low, "and be quiet about it. We gotta move out to keep this place clear. For'd march!" British or Hessian soldiers would have executed the maneuver at attention and marched away smartly in step; the Yankees simply took their places and walked away. This casual approach to discipline had some advantages. American private soldiers in a tight place could think and act as individuals; the rigidly trained Europeans were not allowed to think for themselves. They were expected to act only as ordered.

*   *   *

Naturally, Moses Doan suspected activity at one or another of the ferries. He knew Coryells was out. He stopped by Beaumonts at dusk and found all quiet. It was dark when he reached the shore opposite Mc-Conkeys. He rode cautiously down to the shore. With the wind as it was, he could hear little except occasional thumping sounds. A horse neighed faintly in the distance. He glimpsed a few dim lights that seemed to be lanterns moving on the opposite bank. Something was up all right; he would wait and find out just what it was. He didn't have to wait long. A boatload of soldiers loomed through the falling slurry, and behind it was a double boat loaded with field guns. Mose

left for Trenton, and none too soon. The first boats carried a company of Virginia riflemen instructed to form a cordon around the landing place.

The weather slowed Mose's pace, and it was close to midnight when he reached the town. No doubt he had a password that would get him in. As he passed down King Street, he saw blue Hessian uniforms through lighted windows and heard snatches of German drinking songs and loud bursts of laughter. Colonel Rall's headquarters was guarded as usual, but Mose was told there that the colonel was spending the evening with Abraham Hunt, a wealthy Tory. Doan went to Hunt's and asked for Rall. The colonel sent word by the butler that he was not to be disturbed, so Mose wrote a note. The butler took it to Rall, who, more than a little elevated with wine, stuffed it into his coat pocket without reading it.

*   *   *

Just how General Washington himself crossed the river is not known. Quite possibly it was in a Durham boat, but at least we can be fairly certain that he didn't stand up and strike an attitude in it as the painting shows him doing; he wasn't that kind of a general. McConkey's ferryman, Cadwalader, wrote a memorandum much later saying that he himself rowed Washington and General Knox over in a square-ended bateau. But participation in great events tends to enlarge in retrospect. In any case the general got across. A Captain Fitzgerald, writing up his diary in Slack's ferry house at 3:00 A.M. December 26, reported him as standing on the Jersey shore, wrapped in his cloak, watching the landing of the troops. It was nearly four in the morning when the last boatload got across. Washington had hoped to complete the crossing by midnight, so as to get to Trenton by dawn.

*   *   *

There are green well-kept parks on both sides of the river now. The narrow lane by

94

which the troops left the New Jersey ferry landing is grass-covered, but it is clearly visible, worn a foot deep into the earth. Curiously, it seems the most impressive surviving memorial of the crossing.

*   *   *

When the last boat had landed, Washington mounted a sorrel horse, less conspicuous than his usual gray. He rode forward past the marching men to the head of the long line. At the Bear Tavern, a little over a mile from the landing, the route turned south through the gusting misery. All the men's outer garments were frozen stiff; the ground was slippery; the pace was slow.

About four miles south of the Bear, the route met a crossroad that ran eastward from the New Jersey landing of Yardleys Ferry. Washington, and the larger division under Nathanael Greene, turned left here to the Scotch Road down which they could reach Trenton from the north. General Sulli-

van's division continued another two miles on the original route to reach the River Road, which would bring them into Trenton from the west. These men covered about nine miles from McConkeys Ferry; Greene's men marched more than eleven miles.

In spite of almost unendurable discomfort, the spirits of the men remained high. For once, they were attacking instead of being chased. A few rests were ordered and, as the dark morning wore on, some men fell asleep at every stop. Two who did this never woke again. Had any one been able to report to General Howe what the Americans were doing, he would have refused to believe it— armies simply did not do such insane things. But the wretched, tatterdemalion Yanks trudged on toward Trenton.

As the first gray hint of dawn appeared, a mounted messenger from General Sullivan rode up to the commander. Most of Sullivan's powder had become too wet to fire. Tell the general he will have to attack with bayonets. Another mile. There was a shout at the head of the line. Washington rode forward and met, to his amazement, a company of Virginia infantry. Its captain, no less astonished, reported that he had been sent across on Christmas Day to reconnoiter. His men had recently shot a Hessian sentry! Washington was appalled. Obviously, he would find the alerted Germans ready to oppose him in battle order—but he pressed on; it was too late to do anything else.

Captain Cornelius Coryell announced that the outskirts of Trenton were now only one mile ahead. A chain of whispered orders traveled back along the column and the files broke in to a jogging run, slipping on the ice and sometimes falling, but it was a change and it warmed them up. As they approached a shack, possibly at the intersection of the Dunks Ferry Road, that the general knew was an outpost, there was a shouted challenge in German. The leading company replied to it with a burst of musket fire. The Hessians left the post and retreated in good order, keeping up a covering fire from behind trees and houses. It is doubtful that they realized this was anything more than a raid. It was eight o'clock in the morning. Beyond the shack the Americans, still at the double, fanned out to approach the Princeton Road, which crossed their path and ran along the crest of the valley of Assunpink Creek. Below them, Trenton spread across the slope between the road and the creek.

RISING SUN

13.

Trenton

WASHINGTON, at the top of King Street, could not see through the falling snow as far as the Assunpink bridge. So he couldn't know whether or not Ewing was there on schedule to block it, but he heard musket fire off to the right and knew that some of Sullivan's powder was dry, after all.

Queen Street led up the hill from the bridge to the Princeton Road. King Street, roughly parallel to Queen on the west, also ended at the Princeton Road and so did the street on the east, now called Montgomery. These were the three main streets of Trenton. Up on the hill, General Greene spread his soldiers along the Princeton Road between the ends of the three streets and beyond them. Knox quickly brought up his field guns and placed them, wheel to wheel, across the intersections, aiming down the main streets into the town. Washington sent two regiments into the open fields east of Trenton to cut off escape in that direction.

Sullivan's attack literally woke the town up; it had paid no attention to the firing that attended the retreat of the guards from the outpost. Bleary-eyed Hessians now piled out of their quarters still struggling into their uniforms. No soldier had any idea what was happening, or where his outfit was supposed to assemble—and the officers knew no more than the men. The northeast wind, blowing snow into the faces of the defenders, kept them from seeing clearly the menace north of them, but they knew it was there. Someone, perhaps on command from Colonel Rall, who had rushed outdoors from his quarters, brought two brass fieldpieces into King Street and prepared to shoot them up the hill. A company of infantry began to assemble behind them. Knox loosed a salvo down the street and broke up the muster. Immediately Yankee foot soldiers charged down King Street at a run and captured the two brass guns before they could be fired.

Demoralized Germans piled out of Trenton eastward, to be met by the fire of the American regiments that waited there for them. In utter confusion, the routed soldiers laid down their arms and surrendered. A few Hessians and a platoon of English light horse escaped across the Assunpink bridge moments before Sullivan's men took it. Ewing was still in Pennsylvania; so was Cadwalader; neither had been able to cross the river.

A young officer rode up to General Washington and reported the surrender of the Hessians east of Trenton. The general at once started down the hill toward the center of the town and met a messenger who told him that the rest of the garrison had surrendered, also.

"Huh!" said Sam Baker, "looks like it's all over."

"Not much to it," Ben Taylor said. "I only fired three times and I don't think I hit anything. Might 'a broken somebody's window."

"Ah hit sump'n'! Seen 'im fall over. Y'ole boys jest shoot; Ah shoot *at* sump'n'." Duncan's drawl was unmistakeable.

The sergeant shouted, "Right, *face!* For'd, —march! Col-umn, left!" Then, in a conversational tone: "I reckon we gotta help collect prisoners."

The division moved down the hill and dispersed by platoons into the side streets. The town was quiet; all shooting had stopped. Householders peered furtively from windows and doors. Squads searched every house for hiding enemy soldiers, but the Hessians had not had time to hide. The searchers got glum and fearful receptions in Tory houses; but with the apprehensions of the battle over, the Patriots greeted them ecstatically. When all the Germans had been rounded up and assembled in King Street, there were more than 900 prisoners.

The Yankees next set about counting dead and wounded and also, alas, breaking into Hessian rum kegs against strict orders. Quite a few Americans had wounds, among them Captain William Washington and Lieutenant James Monroe. Astonishingly, no Americans were killed. About thirty Hessians were dead and many were wounded, including

Colonel Rall, who died of his wound later in the day. After his death, it is said, a note was found in his pocket. It read: "Washington is coming on you down the river. He will be here afore long. Doan"

Just when it stopped snowing, if indeed it did stop, isn't recorded. The elation of everybody, whether from joy or rum, was such that no one paid any attention to the weather. They marched back up the river with the prisoners, and with six of the brass field guns and a thousand "stands of arms" (complete fighting equipment for that many men). They also hauled captured ammunition and other supplies back with them in captured wagons drawn by captured horses. There was more ice in the river than there had been the night before, but no one paid any attention to it; they loaded the Durham boats and crossed back into Pennsylvania.

Twenty-three Hessian officers, under guard, stayed overnight in the old Baker ferry house. The rest of the prisoners were marched to Newtown and were sheltered in the Presbyterian Church there. Next day all of them went to Philadelphia, no doubt to be shown off, and then on to the American prison camp at Lancaster, in which town some of their descendants still live. All the uncaptured Hessians in western New Jersey left their posts and retired to the British base at Amboy. General Howe hurriedly sent Cornwallis and a strong force of redcoats to replace them.

Almost as soon as the victory at Trenton was assured, a courier started for Baltimore to report it to Congress. As he passed through Philadelphia, he dropped the story. Newspapers reached the streets as fast as hand presses could turn them out, and also reached the saddlebags of post riders. Within a week the whole country knew about the Battle of Trenton and a renewed wave of patriotic fervor swept the people. George Washington was able to persuade nearly all of his Continentals to reenlist for six additional weeks—at a bonus of ten (paper) Spanish dollars each. And when, on the night of January 1, 1777, he left Cornwallis in Trenton watching campfires on a hill where there was no camp, and marched 5,000 men through the dark to take Princeton, the joy of the country was unbounded.

Within a few weeks the news reached Europe and ministers of state realized for the first time that the Yankee rebellion might be something more than a passing mob scene—that, in fact, this might be the birth of a new nation. To one French minister it occurred that hated England might have her hands full and that France might gain by giving a little quiet help to the revolutionists.

* * *

This is the end of the story. But all true stories are merely bits dipped from the continuing stream of life. Actually, an unimaginable number of stories were happening at the same time; and perhaps what went before, or what came after, might be more interesting than the story that is selected. Who, having read a story to its "end," has not wondered what happened afterward? You know what happened to the Revolutionary War, but if you are curious about what happened at and to the ferry, there is a brief account in the Postscript.

Eagle

Postscript

AFTER Princeton, General Washington, who had left the British at Trenton between his army and his boats, had to move quickly to the heights above Morristown. There the Yankees spent the rest of the winter. Bucks County was left to clean up the mess of the abandoned camps along the Delaware.

Almost overnight, McConkeys Ferry slipped back into its old quiet life, but it shortly changed its name again. After owning it only three years, McConkey sold the ferry, the tavern, and a large acreage to Benjamin Taylor, whom we met as a soldier in Captain van Horn's militia company. So the ferry became Taylors Ferry and continued as that for sixty years. The Taylors,

Quakers all, had lived in Makefield nearly as long as the Bakers had. Ben's grandmother was the daughter of Deborah Booth, who came from England with Henry Baker. Ben's great-grandfather was the uncle of John Wells, who started Wells Ferry.

Coryells Ferry continued to grow as a milling center. In 1784 another Quaker, a wealthy one, Benjamin Parry, bought a gristmill there. He rebuilt it and added a flaxseed mill and a "lumber factory," probably a sawmill. He called his enterprise "Hope Mills." When all his mills burned up six years later, Parry rebuilt them and renamed them "New Hope Mills." The village around them is still New Hope. So much a personage was John Coryell, and so firmly had he stamped his image on the place that, long after his death, many people claimed to have seen his ghost walking through the village, accompanied by *the ghost of his dog, Captain.* The dog was proven a ghost by the fact that cats disregarded him—cats know about ghosts, of course. And by the way, John Coryell's grandson, Young George, moved to Alexandria, Virginia, after the Revolution and became the confidential business agent of George Washington.

The Doans continued their guerilla activities all through the war. In October 1781 they brought off their boldest exploit. By the simple expedient of taking the key away from the Treasurer at gunpoint, they opened the County Treasury at Newtown and cleaned it out. Some sixteen members of the band got $140 apiece in hard money and about as much more in paper. A judge immediately outlawed the Doans and put prices on the heads of the principal members of the band. Anyone giving them aid was to be heavily fined and imprisoned. After that the outlaws had to rob to live, and they terrorized eastern Pennsylvania. All but one of them, who escaped to Canada, were caught eventually. John Tomlinson, and Abraham

and Levi Doan, were hanged. Moses, captured by a posse in a remote cabin, was shot by a nervous vigilante as he lay bound on the floor.

Sam Baker, Jr., lived at Taylors Ferry in the house his grandfather had built, south of the tavern, until 1829. Then he sold the place to Ben Taylor's son Mahlon. That ended the Bakers on the land that their ancestor Henry had settled. The same year, a post office was established in the growing village and the name of the place was officially changed to Taylorsville.

In 1832 the Delaware Division of the Pennsylvania Canal opened from Easton to Bristol, to carry coal and iron down to Philadelphia without shooting the rapids of the river. It passed through the middle of New Hope, but it sheered off below there and passed a little to the west of Taylorsville. At first Durham boats simply went down the canal instead of down the river, but they proved too small for canal traffic and were gradually replaced by standard canal boats pulled by mules. These boats carried a hundred tons of coal. At Bristol they were assembled in flotillas, three boats wide, which sidewheel steamboats towed to Philadelphia. The two Taylor brothers, Mahlon and Bernard, prospered at shipping produce on the canal. Both built large white-painted homes in Taylorsville which still stand.

It is believed that Mahlon also built the stone tavern now known as "The Old Ferry Inn" sometime after 1834, when the covered bridge was opened. It stands on the site of the Bakers' original ferry house, but its entrance is from the filled ramp of the bridge approach, ten or twelve feet higher than the floor of the old taproom.

*   *   *

When the bridge opened, the ferry stopped.

Index

About the Author

EDWIN TUNIS was born in Cold Spring Harbor, New York. He says that his family was peripatetic in his early years; so he attended first grade in a one-room schoolhouse in North Carolina, and later went to schools in Maryland and Delaware. Mr. Tunis studied at the Maryland Institute of Art, and then, for a short period, was a pilot in the U.S. Army Air Service.

Now a designer, illustrator, and muralist of note, he is especially well known for his etchings. The study of American history has always been one of Mr. Tunis' passions, and it was natural for him to combine this interest with his art to produce the distinguished books of American social history for which he is famous. Among these are *Frontier Living*, which was first runner-up for the Newbery Medal; *Colonial Living*, which won the Thomas A. Edison Award; *Oars, Sails, and Steam*, which was chosen by the A.I.G.A. as one of the "Fifty Books of the Year"; *Wheels*, which won the Gold Medal of the Boy's Clubs of America; and *The Young United States 1783–1830*, which was nominated for the National Book Award in 1970.

In addition to social history, Mr. Tunis is also a keen proponent of natural history, as his book *Chipmunks on the Doorstep* delightfully affirms. Mr. Tunis and his wife, who is also an artist, now live in Maryland, not far from Baltimore.